TAROT FOR RELATIONSHIPS

TAROT FOR RELATIONSHIPS

A practical guide to understanding love and sex from Tarot reading

JOCELYN ALMOND and KEITH SEDDON

AQUARIAN

THE AQUARIAN PRESS

First published 1990

British Library Cataloguing in Publication Data

Almond, Jocelyn
Tarot for relationships.
1. Tarot cards
I. Title II. Seddon, Keith
133.3'2424

ISBN 0-85030-850-X

The Aquarian Press is part of the Thorsons Publishing Group, Wellingborough, Northamptonshire, NN8 2RQ, England.

Typeset by Harper Phototypesetters Ltd., Northampton, England.
Printed in Great Britain by Mackays of Chatham, Kent

1 3 5 7 9 10 8 6 4 2

CONTENTS

PREFACE

This book is aimed at the complete newcomer to Tarot as well as the more experienced student. Particular emphasis is placed upon the use of Tarot cards to provide guidance in close personal relationships and sexual relationships, and for each card, as well as a traditional interpretation, we have also given an interpretation which applies specifically to readings concerning someone's love life and relationships. Information on how to do a Tarot card reading, details of spreads for various types of reading, and general meanings for each of the 78 cards are also provided so that the beginner will have all the information needed to be able to give Tarot readings straight away.

Throughout the book we have used the personal pronoun 'he' to stand for the Querent (the person consulting the cards). This is used for convenience and ease of style, and is of course intended to mean 'he or she' in all cases except those few instances where a male Querent is specifically referred to.

Note on the illustrations

The Norse Tarot, designed and drawn by Clive Barrett, has been used to illustrate this book. We have chosen it because it is a fully illustrated deck (that is, it has pictures on the numbered cards of the Minor Arcana). Many modern decks are fully illustrated in this way, and we recommend the use of such a deck for the newcomer to the Tarot because having pictures on all the cards is a very useful aid to their interpretation when giving readings.

CHAPTER ONE

STRUCTURE, PHILOSOPHY AND SYMBOLISM OF THE TAROT

Some books on the Tarot appear daunting to the new student who wants to learn how to read the cards. Full of detailed information on how to treat and store your cards; how to meditate on individual cards; tables and lists of astrological correspondences; parallels with the Hebrew Cabala; and a catalogue of meanings of individual cards which have to be memorized, many of these books are guaranteed to make heavy weather of understanding the Tarot.

Often the advice is quite dogmatic, telling the student that he must learn all this confusing information about the hair and eye colouring and the signs of the zodiac that pertain to each Court card; that he must meditate on the cards, sleep with them and practise every day; that he must understand the basics of the Cabala and memorize the letters of the Hebrew alphabet associated with each card; that he must laboriously memorize any number of signs and symbols, abstract concepts and mythological themes associated with each card, before he can progress to the interesting stage of actually doing a Tarot reading for himself or a friend.

Understandably, many people, when faced with this confusing prospect, try to bypass the process altogether and resort to 'looking up' the meanings of the cards in books that contain lists of meanings whenever they try to do a spread. This tends to reduce the reading to something quite crude and inaccurate, predicting a meeting with a tall dark stranger, a windfall, an unexpected pregnancy, or mysterious good news that is on the way! Reduced to this level, Tarot card reading becomes little more than an amusing game for parties.

Between these two extremes is an approach that gives a basic understanding of the Tarot, and in particular, insight into its underlying principles and guidelines on the actual process of reading a spread; and this is what we try to do in this book. The book is called *Tarot for Relationships* for reasons that will readily become apparent, but we have tried to provide full, basic information on all aspects of the Tarot, not just interpretations relevant to relationships. For each card, a general interpretation, followed by one that is specifically sexual, is provided, but these should not be regarded as setting rigid meanings for the interpretation of the cards. They are intended to help the reader gain insight into ideas that might be associated with the individual cards, and to aid the development of his or her own ideas from that point. It is most important to realize that learning how to use the Tarot is definitely not memorizing 22 upright and 22 reverse meanings of the Major Arcana and 56 upright and 56 reverse meanings of the Minor Arcana; and neither is it a matter of learning a lot of puzzling parallels between the Tarot and astrology and the Cabala, interesting as these topics are to the more advanced practitioner of the Tarot.

Many writers who advocate the complicated approach are basing their teaching on the ideas developed by the Golden Dawn, a secret society for occultists which flourished briefly at the beginning of this century. This attempted to combine together into a single comprehensive philosophy the many different strands of the whole complex and vast area of the Western Tradition of magic. The idea that the Tarot is intimately related to other areas within this Western Tradition is simply a theory that some occultists have espoused, and which others with equal vehemence have denied.

A second and related influence upon the modern views on the Tarot is that of A.E. Waite, who was largely responsible for popularizing the subject at the beginning of this century and who was himself a member of the Golden Dawn. The famous Rider-Waite Tarot deck, which he designed with the help of the artist Pamela Colman Smith, has had a profound effect on the whole subject of Tarot, heavily influencing most, if not all subsequent commentators, and moulding the work of artists and designers who have produced new Tarot decks in the twentieth century. The vast majority of popular modern Tarot decks are closely based upon the Rider-Waite deck.

It is important therefore to bear in mind that there is no single authority on the Tarot. Writers who say that you must do this and you must memorize that, and that each card has this or that specific meaning, are only advocating their own particular view, which probably closely follows Waite and the Golden Dawn, or one of the earlier commentators who has had a similar influence. What is not always apparent is *why* a particular commentator gives that particular interpretation or that particular meaning to the individual cards. As a result it is very confusing to find that different, sometimes contradictory, meanings are given in different books, that some books give reverse meanings and others do not, and that the order and card numbering of the Major Arcana varies from book to book. In fact, some writers have a similar basic view of the cards, but the differences arise from slightly different individual preferences and emphasis. With some writers, on the other hand, the differences arise from a different basic view of the history of the Tarot and the underlying structure of the deck and its symbolism. For instance, someone who believes that the Tarot originated in Egypt is likely to give a different interpretation from someone who believes that it originated in India, or in medieval Europe. There are several important considerations we should take into account, therefore, when we start to look at the Tarot, and paying attention to this will play an important part in understanding *why* we give certain meanings to the cards and *why* we approach a reading in one way rather than another. Briefly, we shall look at these now.

THE MAJOR ARCANA AND THE MINOR ARCANA

The Tarot deck is divided into two parts: the Major Arcana (or Trumps) consisting of 22 cards, and the Minor Arcana consisting of 56 cards. Because of these titles 'Major' and

'Minor', it is often supposed that the former is more important, and some books describe the Major Arcana at great length, while almost totally ignoring the Minor Arcana. When using the cards for divination, however, both groups are of equal importance.

The Major Arcana should be thought of as representing certain fundamental human concepts, principles and basic life experiences which apply to a typical human life. Many of these ideas are cross-cultural, appearing in most or all human societies, while others have importance only in those societies where Tarot cards were developed and used. That is to say, the Major Arcana is concerned with a certain theory of the cosmos or universe, beliefs about birth, marriage, life and death, ethical values, spiritual development, and the relationship of the individual to the world in which he finds himself. The Major Arcana is often presented as a series of moral lessons, progressive life-stages, or steps in a process of initiation into religious or philosophical mysteries. Since the same ideas appear again and again in the religions and myths of the world, these cards can be seen as representing certain mythological themes and characters which have parallels in many cultures. In a Tarot reading, cards of the Major Arcana represent underlying influences, attitudes, and basic themes or ideas in the life of the person for whom the reading is being done.

The Minor Arcana, on the other hand, contains no such fundamental concepts or moral lessons. In the traditional decks, which evolved from medieval times, the 'pip' cards of the Minor Arcana have designs on them similar to those on ordinary playing cards, bearing the appropriate number of suit symbols within a design of leaves or flowers. Modern decks based on the Rider-Waite deck depict scenes which are like illustrations to a story that symbolizes the meaning attached to each card. The Norse Tarot, which illustrates this book, is one such example. The Minor Arcana has four suits of ten pip cards plus four Court cards, and in this respect also resembles decks of modern playing cards (which developed from them), though playing cards have only three Court cards and the suits have different names. In a Tarot reading, the cards of the Minor Arcana represent specific events, incidents, attitudes and people appearing in the life of the person for whom the reading is being done.

In actual practice in a reading, the cards should be freely interpreted, and it is often hard to make a clear distinction between the significance of Major and Minor cards. Generally speaking, however, the Major Arcana can be seen as representing a moral, spiritual or religious reality in a person's life that underlies what is happening to him, while the Minor Arcana represents specific events and experiences.

MASCULINE AND FEMININE

The fundamental categories of male and female, or masculine and feminine, run throughout the Tarot, and in this book we have placed particular emphasis on this aspect. The use of sexual symbolism in the Tarot derives from the ancient belief that everything in creation is either masculine or feminine, or is produced from either a union or a conflict between the two. Many creation myths present a sexual interpretation of how the world came into being; for example, that it was produced from the sexual union of a male and female deity or that it issues from the womb of a maternal goddess. This kind of explanation pre-dates the creation myths prevalent in patriarchal religious belief with which Christians are more familiar. However, the ancient symbolism still persists within folk culture and appears very conspicuously in the Tarot.

The four suits of the Minor Arcana, for instance, are marked by symbols which represent male and female sexual organs — Wands and Swords are phallic symbols and Cups and Discs are womb symbols. Consequently, Wands and Swords are to be regarded as masculine suits while Cups and Discs are feminine suits, and meanings are traditionally attributed to the cards on this basis. In the Major Arcana most of the cards depict either a male or a female figure and many of these represent the different aspects of what are known as the masculine principle and the feminine principle.

The masculine principle is characterized by positive, energetic, assertive, rational and creative qualities, while the feminine principle involves negative, passive, nurturing, mysterious, emotional and non-rational qualities. This may be immediately suspect to someone living in our Western culture in the late twentieth century when such notions appear simplistic or even sexist, apparently embodying sexual stereotypes which are currently being questioned and undermined. We should recognize, however, that when we are talking about 'masculine' and 'feminine' in this context we are not describing what actual men and women are really like. The masculine and feminine principles, as they arise in ancient philosophies, are directly opposing ideals; they are mutually exclusive categories, each defined in terms of qualities that exclude the other, and apparently based upon concepts derived from male and female biology. The male penis is seen as active, hard and penetrating, while the female vagina is seen as passive, soft and yielding, and the female womb is receptive and nurturing towards the developing foetus.

Central to the whole philosophy contained in the Tarot is the idea of tension, conflict, union and balance which arises between these equal but opposite principles of masculine and feminine. The idea is that qualities pertaining to both male and female are manifested within each person, every relationship, every situation, every experience, and indeed within the very structure of the cosmos itself. The notion of male superiority and female inferiority is completely alien to the philosophy of the Tarot. The whole idea of a tension and balance between the two opposing forces or principles of masculinity and femininity depends upon those opposing forces being equal and complementary to one another and would be utterly undermined if we were to think of one as being superior to or better than the other. Indeed, according to this view, the masculine and feminine principles need one another in order for completeness and full potential to be attained. In Eastern Tantric philosophy, the power of the god is invested in his female consort or Shakti, without which he is powerless. In the philosophy of the Hebrew Cabala there is a corresponding idea, the power of God being in his Shekina — his female soul or divine consort. Similarly, the prevalence of sexual symbolism in Eastern religious art was intended to represent the sacred mystery of the union of the masculine and feminine principles, but unfortunately to prurient Western eyes it has often been interpreted on a purely mundane level and hence regarded as primitive, crude or even obscene.

Corresponding to the masculine principle are important symbols and concepts which recur throughout the Tarot. The sun and the clockwise motion traditionally associated with it, the world of daylight, life, earthly power and ambition, rationality, intellect, and qualities we can characterize as those of the extroverted personality, are all contained within the masculine principle. Likewise, the moon, anti-clockwise motion, the mysterious world of night, the unconscious, the life of the spirit and the emotions, psychic power, introspection, the unknown, and the mysteries of death and the afterlife, are all contained within the concept of the feminine principle. Recognizing this as one of the fundamental themes of the Tarot does much to explain why certain meanings are attached to certain cards.

When we look at the Major Arcana, for instance, it is immediately apparent that many of the cards can be categorized as male and female, according to the above guidelines. Likewise, many of the characteristics of masculinity or femininity can instantly be attached to that card to give it its meaning, even by someone who has only this rudimentary knowledge of the Tarot.

It may be noted that the categorization of the cards into male or female is roughly half and half; neither gender predominates. Of the four Court cards in each suit of the Minor Arcana, three appear to be male (the Page, the Knight and the King) and one female, but in order that there should be two of each sex, the Page of each suit is often regarded as female, and in some decks is called the Princess. Some other decks follow this idea by renaming the Court cards to make two of them female, and this is the case with the Norse Tarot. Clive Barrett, in his handbook for this deck, explains that he has renamed the Knights as Princesses, and the Pages as Princes. However, since most commentators when selecting one of the male Court cards to be female choose the Page for this purpose, we have decided to follow the more usual practice in this book and have accordingly identified the Prince with the Knight of each suit, and the Page with the Princess.

THE ELEMENTS

It was an ancient belief that everything in the universe consisted of four elements and that different substances were made up of different quantities of these four elements combined together. These elements were Earth, Air, Fire and Water, and when they were manifested in a human being they were called *humours* and were supposed to determine the physical characteristics and psychological temperament of that person. Thus someone displaying certain distinctive physical features and certain character traits would be supposed to have a predominance of a particular humour or element in his body and psychological make-up. Furthermore, the four elements were subsumed under the two categories of male and female — Fire and Air being male, and Water and Earth being female.

These ideas, again, are fundamental to the Tarot. The four suits of the Minor Arcana are thought to represent these four elements and their corresponding humours: Wands represent Fire, Cups represent Water, Swords represent Air, and Discs represent Earth. Thus the distinctive qualities of each element permeate the suit which represents that element, and the psychological qualities and physical appearance pertaining to each of the humours attaches to the relevant Court cards of each suit. This explains the reasoning behind the meanings and personalities traditionally ascribed to the cards of the Minor Arcana.

ETERNITY AND CYCLES OF EXISTENCE

The concept of eternity, of recurring cycles of birth, life and death, creation and destruction, is another concept fundamental to the philosophy of the Tarot. In our modern Western, Christian-based, materialistic culture, we tend to believe in a single linear process that starts with a birth or beginning and ends in death or destruction, and within the span between there is ideally a growth or progress, building on what went before. We tend to view an individual life and the history of the world along these lines. Such notions as cosmic cycles and reincarnation do not generally prevail, and many people no longer believe in life after death. The idea of creation being cyclic is associated with Eastern religion and philosophy rather than the traditions of the West. In understanding the Tarot, however, we must accept this Eastern cosmology contained within it.

The infinity symbol ∞, called a lemniscate, occurs several times in the designs of the cards in most Tarot decks. You will find it above the heads (or incorporated into the hats) of the Magician and Strength (or Fortitude) in many traditional decks and in modern decks based on the Rider-Waite. In traditional decks it often appears in the design around the two Disc symbols on the Two of Discs, and also appears in the Rider-Waite pictorial design of that same card. In the Major Arcana, The Wheel of Fortune and The World cards both have circular designs, and the meanings associated with them are based on the idea of cosmic cycles, change and destiny, death and rebirth. We should bear in mind, therefore, that in the philosophy of the Tarot, every ending is also a beginning and every death is a prelude to rebirth.

Interestingly, we can lay out the 22 cards of the Major Arcana in the form of an infinity symbol, as in the diagram on the next page.

In drawing the lemniscate, it will be seen that it consists of two circles: one male/clockwise/solar circle representing the masculine principle, and one female/anti-clockwise/lunar circle representing the feminine principle. When the cards are placed in this pattern, the circular designs of The Wheel and The World occur at the intersection. The cards of the male circle turn outwards, symbolizing extroversion, activity and interaction with the physical world, while those of the female circle turn inwards symbolizing introspection, passivity, and the cultivation of psychic qualities. The cards of the male circle are numbered clockwise 0 to 9 (single figures) and the cards of the female circle are numbered anti-clockwise 11 to 20 (double figures).

Many commentators have seen a correspondence in terms of meaning between the cards of one circle and their 'opposite' or 'complementary' number in the other circle. For instance, we might pair The Fool with Judgement, The

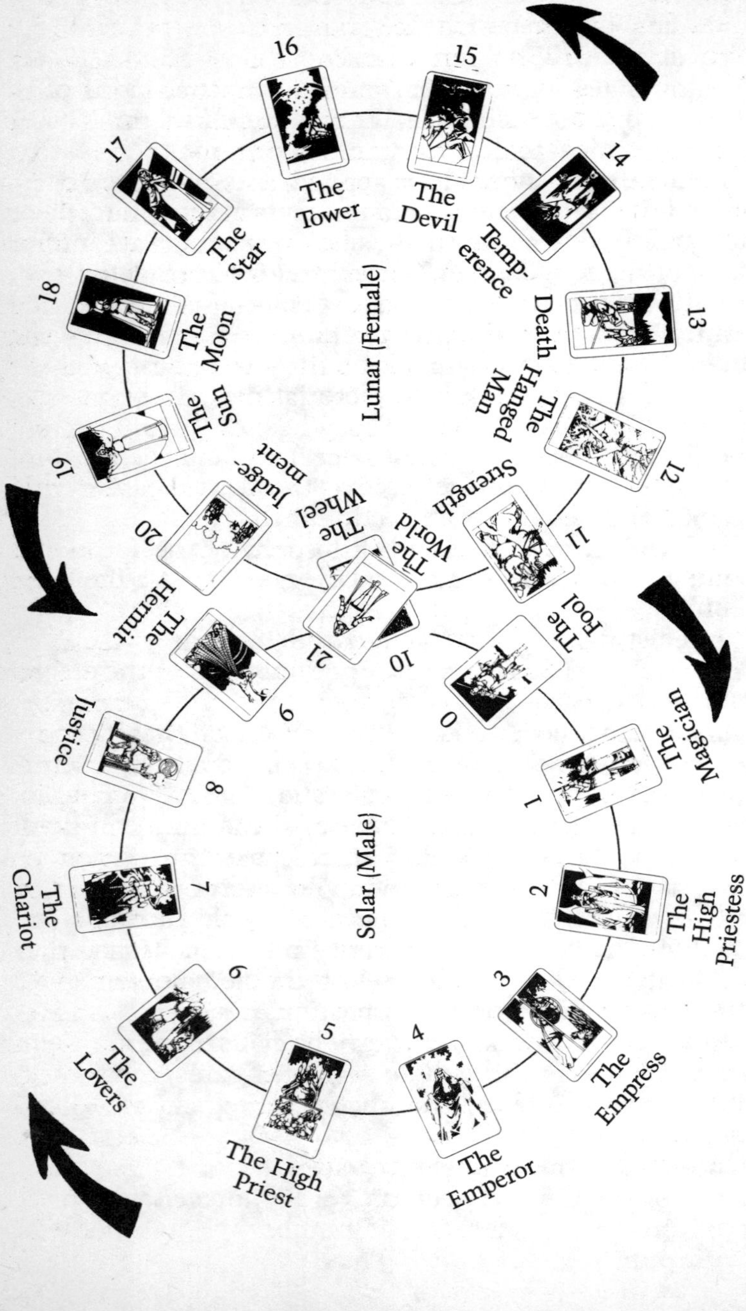
Lunar (Female)
Solar (Male)
0 The Fool
1 The Magician
2 The High Priestess
3 The Empress
4 The Emperor
5 The High Priest
6 The Lovers
7 The Chariot
8 Justice
9 The Hermit
10 The Wheel
11 Strength
12 The Hanged Man
13 Death
14 Temp-erence
15 The Devil
16 The Tower
17 The Star
18 The Moon
19 The Sun
20 Judge-ment
21 The World

Magician with The Sun, The High Priestess with The Moon, The Empress with The Star, and so on; or we might, alternatively, pair the cards marked 1 and 11, 2 and 12, 3 and 13, 4 and 14, and so on. The meanings attached to the pairs of cards can be seen to be complementary, similar, or opposed, according to the various interpretations that different commentators have applied; and again, laying the cards out in this way and trying to find these correspondences will help the newcomer to Tarot understand the reasoning behind the interpretations that are often applied to the different cards. For instance, the conceptual relationship between the masculine, extrovert, energetic Magician, and the masculine, powerful, radiating energy of the Sun, is a fairly obvious point, and typical of Tarot symbolism and philosophy; as is the conceptual relationship between the feminine, introspective, mysterious High Priestess or Papess and the feminine, pale mysterious, eerie Moon.

Other correspondences may be less obvious, but an attempt to find them is often the basis for the meaning attached to the various cards. For instance, if we follow the system that pairs The Magician with The Sun, The High Priestess with The Moon and The Empress with The Star, then The Emperor corresponds to The Tower. The Emperor, representing a masculine archetype, stands for worldly power and authority; while The Tower, on the other hand, can be seen as a man-made construction in the form of a phallic symbol which is struck down by a thunderbolt from heaven, plunging its inhabitants (one of which is sometimes shown wearing a crown) to their destruction. Thus we might draw a moral lesson from this to the effect that worldly authorities and institutions which arrogantly challenge the laws of divine justice and authority will ultimately be destroyed. Other writers have commented on these ideas, and it is unnecessary to elaborate upon them here, but it may be helpful for the student of Tarot to bear in mind that such correspondences have been found and that attempting to make them may be helpful in understanding and learning the cards.

THE SIGNIFICATOR

Some Tarot readers choose a card to represent the Querent (i.e., the person for whom the reading is being done) or, occasionally, the issue that the reading concerns. The card that plays this role is called the Significator.

The Significator, when it represents the Querent, is usually one of the Court cards, and is chosen on the basis of the Querent's sex, age, and astrological sign or physical appearance. Kings represent mature men, Queens represent mature women, Princes (or Knights) represent young men, and Princesses (or Pages) represent young women or children of either sex. Astrological signs, like the suits of the Tarot, are categorized according to the four elements; so someone born under a Fire sign, for instance, would have a Significator chosen from the Wands suit, and someone born under an Earth sign would have the Significator chosen from the Discs suit, and so forth. Alternatively, the Significator can be chosen on the basis of hair and eye colouring. People with blonde or red hair are represented by Wands; people with light brown hair and blue or hazel eyes are represented by Cups; those with dark brown hair are represented by Swords; and those with black or white hair, or members of the dark-skinned races, are represented by Discs.

It is perfectly possible to do a reading without a Significator, however, which is the approach we take in this book in the chapter about how to do a reading. Although some Tarot readers say that choosing the Significator helps to concentrate the mind on the Querent and to give focus to the reading, in our experience this is unnecessary, and has the disadvantage of removing one card from the deck which could have been of use had it naturally been one of the cards to turn up in the spread. The card which represents the Querent can usually be recognized if it appears in the spread as a matter of course, and the position in which it turns up and whether it is upright or reversed will provide helpful insights which would have been lost had this card been removed at the outset.

DIGNITY OF CARDS IN A TAROT SPREAD

As mentioned earlier, doing a Tarot reading is not, as it often appears to be, simply a matter of memorizing particular meanings of the cards and reciting the meaning of each card as it comes up in a spread. When doing a reading, the cards should not be seen as distinct items, each one bearing its own meaning, but rather the meaning should be derived from the whole arrangement and layout of the cards that come up in a spread. The position and relationship of the cards, and whether they are upright or reversed, is as important as the general meaning attached to each individual card.

An important point to be considered is the significance of reversed cards. A card is said to be reversed when, after the appropriate shuffling and laying out of the cards in a spread, it is upside down from the point of view of the Tarot card reader. (If the Querent — the person for whom the reading is being done — is sitting on the opposite side of the table, he will see the whole spread upside down.) The terms 'upright' and 'reversed' are applied according to the reader's viewpoint. Some commentators on the Tarot disregard reversed meanings altogether, turning the cards upright should they accidentally be laid reversed. It has become increasingly accepted, however, that if a card appears reversed then this is significant and should be taken into account, so most Tarot readers shuffle the deck in such a way as to ensure that some cards will be reversed.

However, the significance of a reversed card is not generally agreed upon, which accounts for an even greater discrepancy between reverse meanings given in different books than between upright meanings. In this book we have suggested reverse meanings that are largely negative or worse than upright meanings, on the principle that pictures are meant to be seen upright and that intuitively there seems to be something wrong or unfortuitous about a picture which is upside down. A disadvantage of this approach is that it may have the effect of making a greater number of unpleasant meanings, since some upright meanings are unfortunate as well. In actual practice, however, we have not found that this approach produces abnormally pessimistic or negatively-biased readings.

Other writers on the Tarot would strongly object to reverse meanings being bad or negative, preferring to give reverse meanings that are simply the reverse of upright meanings, so that a card with an unfortunate upright meaning would lose its unpleasant characteristics and take on a far better meaning when reversed. All this only goes to show that anyone's Tarot reading technique is largely a matter of personal taste and that the student should take the approach that seems most appealing and intuitively right. There are no hard and fast rules here.

Another important point with regard to the 'dignity' of the cards is their bearing upon one another. Some commentators describe a card as being 'well-dignified' or 'ill-dignified' according to the meaning of adjacent cards. Thus the unfortunate meaning of one card will be lessened by surrounding cards which have a favourable meaning, while the fortunate meaning of another card will be lessened by the influence of the unfortunate meanings of surrounding cards.

It should therefore be noted that individual cards do not have a rigidly fixed meaning, because the meaning is subtly altered by the particular spread that is being used and by the position of the cards in that spread. In the following chapter we provide a selection of spreads that can be used for answering a range of different kinds of question, and we give some general hints on how to approach a Tarot reading.

CHAPTER TWO
DOING A TAROT READING

To many people, Tarot card reading is a foolish, superstitious practice with no possible rational basis. There appears to be no normal causal explanation for why the meanings suggested in the cards should have any bearing at all, in the manner that they are purported to do, upon the life and experiences of the person for whom the reading is being done.

If there is a connection, it seems to be in terms of a *meaningful coincidence*, or what the psychologist Carl Jung called 'synchronicity'. Tarot card reading, like any form of divination, is a method of deriving meaning from happenings which are seemingly random or chance occurrences. At the root of this there is of course the belief that chance occurrences are not really chance at all; that some underlying, meaningful, acausal ordering principle is at work, and that given the right circumstances (i.e., by elimination of many of the normal causal connections) this underlying order and meaning will become apparent.

It is for this reason that ritual practices and behaviour are an intrinsic part of Tarot card reading, for they help to put both the reader and the Querent in the appropriate frame of mind and create the right conditions in which a symbolic order can be created out of apparent chaos. Consequently, many books on the Tarot recommend certain requirements for keeping and using the cards, methods of shuffling and choosing cards, elaborate methods of dealing or counting them out, and so on. As with the points mentioned earlier, however, it is largely a matter of personal choice. The important thing to remember is that the same method should be used on each occasion, so that the process becomes automatic as a fixed procedure that is common to each reading and provides the unchanging background against which the apparently random selection of cards acquires a meaning that is unique on each occasion.

The following points, therefore, should be observed.

KEEPING AND USING THE DECK CORRECTLY

Always use your own deck and do not allow other people to play with it or to handle it, except in the context of doing a reading for them. The reason for this is often said to be that the deck becomes 'contaminated' with other people's psychic vibrations and fails to work properly. For a similar reason, Tarot readers are sometimes advised to sleep with their cards under their pillow, so as to 'charge up' the deck with their own psychic vibrations.

Whether such esoteric explanations are accepted or not, it is preferable to treat your cards with care and respect, to handle them and lay them out only when learning how to use them and when actually doing a reading. This helps to cultivate the frame of mind most conducive to doing a good reading, whereas a casual or careless attitude in this respect is unlikely to do so.

Make sure that the deck you are using suits your personal taste. If you are trying to make do with one you do not really like, you are unlikely to do good readings. Always use your own deck and not one which is second-hand or belongs to someone else. When not in use, wrap the cards up in a silk scarf or handkerchief and keep them in a wooden box if you have one that is suitable. When doing a reading, it is also helpful to lay out the cards on a special cloth that is used exclusively for the purpose. Again, a silk cloth is preferable though this may seem an unnecessary expense to the new student; otherwise a cloth of any plain material would be suitable, though it should ideally be a dark colour or black. The purpose of the cloth is to provide a good surface on which the cards can be kept clean and seen clearly without external distractions, even when a reading is being done in unfamiliar surroundings. Silk is traditionally used for wrapping and laying the cards on because it is thought to be a good psychic insulator, protecting them from the influence of other people's psychic vibrations. Whether this explanation is accepted or not, taking such measures helps to promote the right attitude and provides a feeling of familiarity and confidence when using the cards.

SHUFFLING AND SELECTION OF CARDS FOR A SPREAD

The Tarot reader and the Querent should sit facing one another across the table. If a Significator is being used, this should be removed from the deck at the start of the reading and laid to one side. The reader shuffles the cards first, turning some of the cards round if reverse meanings are being included. The deck should then be handed to the Querent to shuffle.

When the Querent returns the cards to the reader, it is important to note which way up they are handed back. The reader should assume that the cards are given to him or her the right way up for the reading, and thus the reader should *not* turn them the other way round. Whenever the cards are handed to the reader at any point during the reading, care should always be taken not to turn the cards upside down. If the Querent turns the cards upside down, however, this should be taken as part of his or her choice as to which way up the cards should be read. If the Querent hands the cards back sideways, the reader should ask which is to be regarded as the top.

The cards for the reading are now to be selected. This can be done in a number of ways. One method is for the reader to spread out the deck face down and ask the Querent to select the required number of cards, keeping them in the order that they are chosen. If the Querent makes a pile of the chosen cards, the reader should take note whether the top card is the first or the last one chosen, and lay out the spread accordingly, laying the card first chosen in position one, the second card in position two, and so on. Again, if the Querent muddles up the cards in choosing them, assume this is part of the choice and carry on regardless. The important point is that the reader should not muddle the cards or turn them round after the Querent's choice has been made.

A second method of selecting the cards is to ask the Querent to cut the deck after it has been shuffled. This should be done as follows: using the left hand, the Querent should cut the deck once, making a second pile to the left of the first, and the second pile itself should then be cut, making a third pile which is laid to the left of the other two. The deck is then reassembled, putting the first pile on top of the second and both on top of the third, so that what was previously on the top of the deck is now on the bottom. The reader now deals the appropriate number of cards off the top of the deck.

Other methods of selection may be used for particular spreads, and for some it may be necessary to separate the Major and Minor Arcana before making the selection. Whichever method you use is a matter of personal choice, but it is best to keep to the same method on each occasion once you have found one that you like.

LAYING OUT THE SPREAD

The reader lays out the cards *face down* in the pattern of the spread. The first card chosen should be put in position one, the second card in position two, and so on, according to the diagram of the chosen spread. (We provide a selection of spreads in the next chapter.) The reader should always take care to keep the cards in the order they were handed to him or her by the Querent, and not to reverse or muddle them.

When the cards are correctly laid out they should then be turned over, a few at a time as the reading progresses, or all together at the start of the reading. Do not try to turn over the cards as you lay them out, because this can cause confusion — it is best to take one step at a time. As before, they should not be reversed at this stage. Turn them over from side to side and *not* from top to bottom, which would turn them upside down.

As already mentioned, the cards are to be regarded as upright or reversed from the reader's point of view.

INTERPRETING THE SPREAD

The reader's first step in interpreting the spread should be to look for an overall theme or atmosphere. A predominance of a particular suit, of Major cards, of Minor cards, or of Court cards, is significant. For instance, if there are many Major Arcana cards, this could indicate that the Querent is going through a period of major life changes or events that are largely outside his control. A predominance of Court cards suggests that a number of other people are closely involved in the Querent's affairs at the present time. A predominance of Wands may indicate that career and business affairs are uppermost in the Querent's mind, whereas a predominance of Cups would suggest that his love life, sex, and relationships are an important concern at this time. Discs suggest domestic matters, physical pleasure, money and emotional security or insecurity. Many reversed cards or cards of the Swords suit indicate problems, obstacles, broken relationships and worries in general.

The general atmosphere of the spread can thus be seen at a glance, and the reading should be carried through consistently with reference to this first impression. The student should attempt from the start to see the spread as a whole rather than as an array of individual cards.

The second step is to take note of the meaning ascribed to each position in the spread. Look at the cards representing the past and future; is there an improvement or a decline in circumstances? Look for the major problem areas. Do they focus in a particular area of the Querent's life, such as family, personal health, etc? If there is a position in the spread that represents a solution to the problem, or an outcome, is this advice helpful? Try to get a general impression of what the spread is saying before looking in more detail at the individual meanings of the cards.

The third step is to start to describe what is meant by each card as it appears in that particular position. This can be done by starting with card number one and going on to cards numbered two, three, four, and so on, until the end. Alternatively, the reader might focus on a particular card which appears important or central to the overall meaning of the spread, and interpret the other cards in the light of this one which seems of special importance. Intuition and experience of doing readings will help the student to acquire this second approach, which may be a little more difficult at first.

Finally, the reading should be summed up, pointing out the major findings, possible solutions to problems, and advice where appropriate. Again, a special attempt should be made here to see the spread as a whole and not as an array of cards with various and conflicting meanings. The total spread should appear coherent and consistent, and if one or two cards seem anomalous or inconsistent, the reader should attempt to give an alternative interpretation of these cards to make them fit in better with the spread as a whole. At first sight this may seem like cheating or distorting the meaning to fit the facts; but this is not the case. It should be viewed rather as an intuitive, creative exercise and an attempt to find helpful, meaningful answers to the Querent's current problems, using a system of random association, suggestion and intuition to throw up solutions which may previously not have been thought of.

In this book we have placed emphasis on the sexual symbolism in the Tarot and have provided interpretations of each card which will enable the Tarot reader to give readings with an orientation towards the love life or sex life of the Querent. In placing this emphasis we do not mean to suggest that the aspects of the Querent's life concerning relationships should be stressed more than any other aspect; however, relationships, love and sexual fulfilment are likely to be important in most people's lives, and people frequently consult a Tarot reader on matters of this nature. In fact it would be very odd if a question regarding love, marriage or a close personal relationship did not arise at some point during most readings, as these topics are frequently central to people's lives.

In providing the interpretations for relationships we also hope to show how the general or traditional meaning of each card may be adapted to fit a particular situation — in this case, a situation concerning the Querent's love life and relationships. Obviously it will not always be appropriate to interpret the cards in this way, either to give the interpretation for relationships or to recite a rigid traditional meaning which is inappropriate to the individual reading. As we have already stressed, it is up to the reader to interpret the cards intuitively and to develop, with practice, his or her own personal meanings for each card.

CHAPTER THREE
SOME USEFUL SPREADS

To explain in more detail how to approach an actual reading, it is now necessary to look at particular spreads. It is advisable for the beginner to start with simple spreads that use only a few cards and which have only one card in each position, before progressing to complex spreads involving many cards (sometimes the entire deck) and which have three or more cards in each position in the spread.

The more experienced Tarot reader will use different spreads for different purposes. For instance, a spread which has a number of positions dealing with many different areas of the Querent's life can be used to gain a general view of the Querent's personality and present circumstances, while other smaller spreads are more suited to answering specific questions, for looking in detail at one particular area of the Querent's life or one major problem on which advice is sought.

THE HORSESHOE SPREAD

The spread we shall look at first is a simple five-card spread which is suitable either for a brief general view of the Querent's situation, or for examining one specific problem.

After the shuffling and selection procedure has been completed, the cards are laid out in the horseshoe shape as shown in the diagram. You may ask, why lay the cards out like this rather than in a straight line? A similar question could be asked of any of the spreads or layouts. The answer is that the pattern of the cards in the layout is important in seeing more clearly the contrasts and comparisons that can

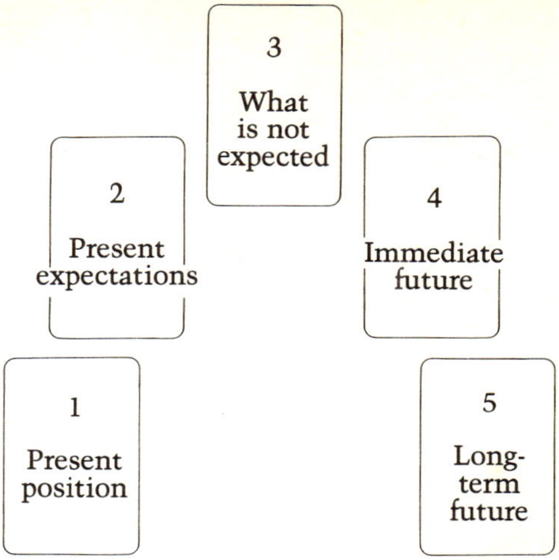

The Horseshoe Spread

be made between the individual cards. This particular spread places the cards representing the present on one side, and the cards representing the future on the other, suggesting that certain enlightening comparisons may be made between the opposing cards. The card in the middle, labelled 'What is not expected' being placed at the top, stands out as particularly significant because of its positioning. This arrangement should give the Tarot reader a clue as to how to interpret the spread.

Often the position labelled 'The unexpected' or 'What is not expected' is particularly puzzling to the new student of Tarot who may not know whether to interpret the card that comes up in this position as showing an actual future event, a possible future event, or something that is unlikely to happen at all. In fact this card may be especially useful, suggesting a solution to the Querent's problem that he had previously overlooked or dismissed; it may offer an alternative course of action to that which the Querent was planning or expecting to take. It may, alternatively, show an unforseen obstacle.

When reading this spread, therefore, it will be helpful to interpret cards 2 and 3 with reference to one another, showing, if possible, the contrast between what the Querent expects (card number 2) and an alternative possible course of action, solution, or obstacle, that he does not expect (card number 3). Both these cards should be interpreted in turn with reference to card number 1, his present position or circumstances.

The cards numbered 4 and 5 can be seen as showing the immediate outcome and the more long-term effects of any decision that the Querent makes now. Again, cards 4 and 5 should be interpreted in the light of cards numbered 2 and 3. Does the future or likely outcome tally more closely with what the Querent expects or with what he does not expect? Does card number 3 suggest some unexpected course of action which could lead to a favourable outcome shown in cards 4 or 5? On the other hand, card number 3 could indicate an unexpected obstacle or problem which may lead to unfavourable circumstances shown in cards 4 and 5. Pointing out these possible problems to the Querent will hopefully help him to avoid them.

THE CELTIC CROSS SPREAD

The second spread we shall look at is the Celtic Cross, which is a very popular spread described in many books on the Tarot. The advantage of this spread is that it enables one to look at a particular problem, or at the Querent's present situation and future prospects, from a number of different angles, examining not only the actual events which have happened or are likely to happen in the future, but also the underlying influences which give rise to those events.

Card number 1 shows the Querent's present situation or may show some matter that the Querent is concerned about at this time. Card number 2 is laid across it, and should be interpreted as if it were upright. This may seem to present a problem in interpretation if the card happens to be one with a fortunate meaning that can scarcely be construed as an obstacle. It should be remembered, however, that the cards should always be read in combination with one another. Cards 1 and 2 therefore should be seen as different aspects of the same situation, and the combination of them may show conflicts and problems which are not apparent when the cards are seen in isolation from one another. These cards in turn should be compared with the surrounding cards.

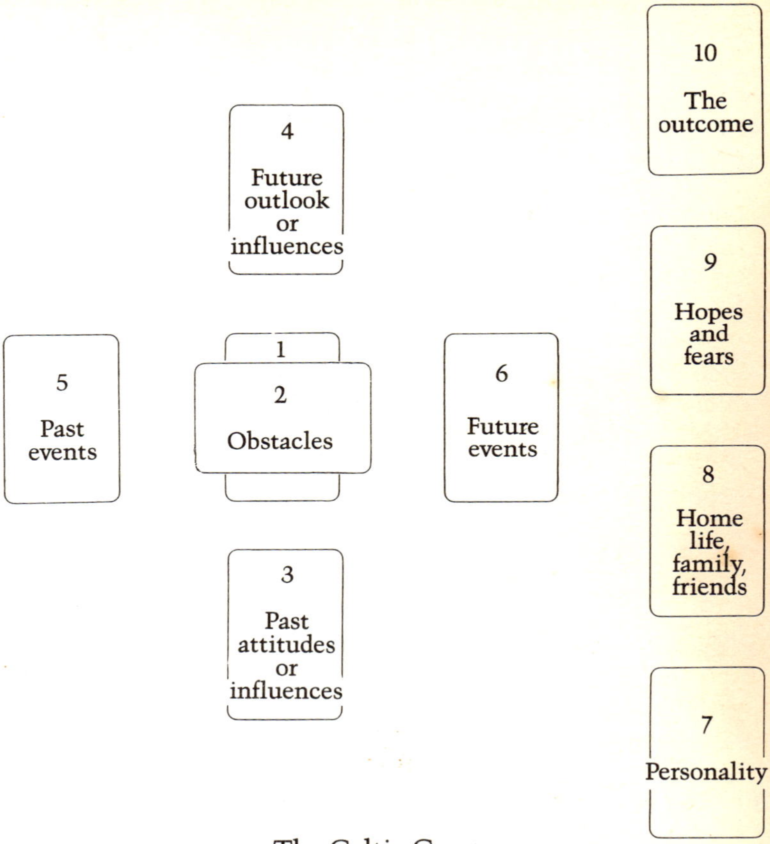

The Celtic Cross

It may thus be seen that even a fortunate card could represent an obstacle or difficulty in the context of other less fortunate cards in the spread, and in fact the more negative and unpleasant the whole spread appears, the more absurd it would be to interpret a card such as The Sun or The World that happened to appear in the position of 'Obstacles' as having its usual fortunate upright meaning. If we suppose, for instance, that the other cards included the Three of Swords, the Ten of Swords, The Devil, and a number of reversed cards conveying unfortunate meanings, should The Sun happen to appear in the position of 'Obstacles' it would be ludicrous to say that the Querent had no obstacles or problems confronting him, given the general atmosphere of the rest of the spread. In such a situation, the obvious discrepancy between a card such as The Sun and the general pessimistic atmosphere of the rest of the spread may well suggest that a major problem for the Querent is the gulf between his aims and ideals and the actual circumstances in which he presently finds himself.

Of course, there may always be cases where one would want to say that the Querent has no particular obstacles or difficulties, but again, the cards in the rest of the spread would be used to support this view.

Card number 3 is labelled 'Past attitudes or influences' which is not to be confused with card number 5, 'Past events'. The usual interpretation of these positions is to say that card number 5 shows events and experiences which are in the past and which are now ceasing to influence the Querent. They are often described as being 'behind him' in the sense of no longer being a direct part of his life or present concerns. Card number 3, on the other hand, shows attitudes and influences which may not only have been the underlying cause of those past events, but which may still be influencing the Querent now. Card number 3, for instance, may show some aspect of the Querent's own personality or the influence of other people which has motivated his past actions and which is responsible for his present situation as well.

Card number 4 shows future influences on the Querent's life in much the same way as card number 3 showed past influences. It is useful, however, to compare these two cards to see if any change of attitude or direction is indicated for the future. Card number 4 can also be interpreted in a similar way to card number 3 in the previous spread which represented 'What is not expected'. In this spread, card number 4 may show a future influence or change in the Querent's own attitude, the possibility of which has not until now been recognized. Thus card number 4 could draw attention to possible future trends in the Querent's life which he has not yet consciously considered.

When interpreting the remaining cards it is important to refer back to the earlier cards, making, for instance, a comparison between cards number 4 and number 9, and cards number 10 and number 6. Card number 9 shows the Querent's hopes and fears, while card number 4, showing future possible influences, may help to put these hopes and fears into clearer perspective. Card number 7 shows the Querent's own personality and attitudes, while card number 8 shows the attitudes and influences of those around him, or the quality of his relationships with them.

Card number 10, 'The outcome', may at first sight appear to represent simply a future event which will result from present circumstances. However, this card can also be seen as a helpful way of summing up the whole spread, and may to some extent be interpreted as an overview of the entire situation shown in the rest of the cards. Thus, an apparently unfortunate card appearing in that position, such as The Tower, would not necessarily point to some future disaster, but could be a way of characterizing the general atmosphere of the whole spread, indicating that the Querent may at present be experiencing a time of shattered illusions and disappointments, but that in the future the whole experience will be seen as worthwhile and illuminating in retrospect.

NINE-CARD SPREAD

The next spread we shall look at, the Nine-Card Spread, is particularly useful in clarifying the Querent's situation and for locating the areas of his life that may be especially problematic. It will be noted that only one card is allocated to the past and only one to the future, so this spread is not very useful for predicting the outcome of a situation. It will be more useful as an introductory spread for gaining a general view of the Querent's situation before progressing to other spreads which may answer specific questions or deal with one particular area of concern.

It will be seen in this spread that the middle row of cards (2, 5 and 8) deals with the Querent's own personality and his relationship with other people. Although card number 5 can loosely be described as representing 'Family', while card number 8 represents 'Acquaintances', it is frequently the case that a person's relationships cannot be so neatly categorized. Self-employed people, for instance, may be working at home, or their home life and business life may be closely connected. Some people may have more intimate

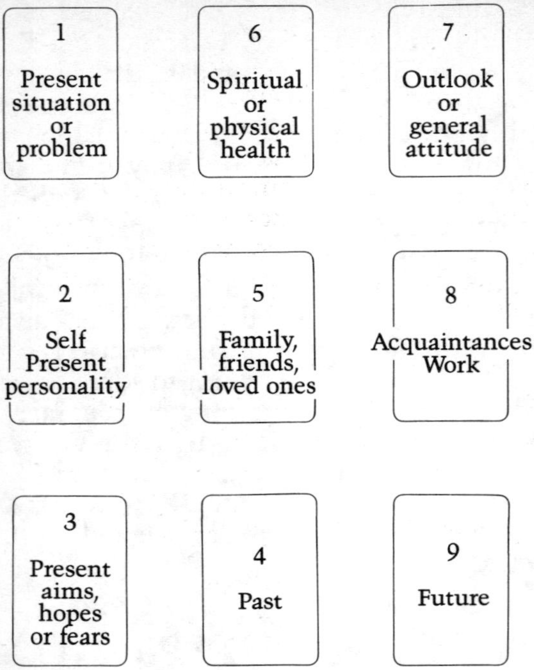

Nine-Card Spread

relationships with their friends than with their family. It may be more accurate, therefore, to view position number 5 as showing the Querent's more intimate relationships, while position number 8 indicates casual acquaintances or a work situation outside the home. Often, however, there is no clear distinction between cards number 5 and 8, which may simply show different aspects of the same relationship.

With regard to cards number 3 and 7, they may tend to refer to the same psychological features of the Querent. In general it could be said that card number 7 shows prevailing or long-term psychological characteristics, or an attitude that is generally part of the Querent's personality. Number 3, on the other hand, shows present attitudes which may be temporary and possibly related to the situation shown in card number 1.

Card number 6 should perhaps be mentioned in particular as its interpretation may prove difficult. The card in this position can show the spiritual or physical health of the Querent; however, the interpretation is often unhelpful or inappropriate unless the Querent happens to have some marked or significant health problem. Of course, if the Querent should be concerned with some health matter or a deep psychological problem, this is the position in the spread where such a problem would show up. An alternative way of viewing card number 6 is to interpret it rather like card number 10 (The Outcome) in the previous spread, in that it can give an overview of the whole spread or back up points which are indicated in other areas of the spread.

By saying that a spread, like the individual cards, should not be interpreted in a fixed or rigid way, it may seem to create even more uncertainty and confusion, which is not our intention. The positions in the spread are intended to give guidance in interpreting the individual cards, narrowing down the area of the Querent's life to which a particular card applies and so enabling the Tarot reader to decide upon the most appropriate interpretation of the card in the context of that particular reading. Sometimes, however, a rigid interpretation of the position in the spread, or of the individual cards, will be inappropriate, and so the reader should always be prepared to take a flexible approach, using the designated positions in the spread to suggest the right interpretation of the cards whenever possible, but also using intuition to abandon this method and interpret the cards more freely whenever this seems appropriate.

THE 21-CARD SPREAD

The fourth spread may prove more difficult for the newcomer to Tarot to interpret, as each position has three cards, rather than simply one. Experience gained from relating the cards together in the earlier spreads, which have only one card in each position, should now be employed in understanding this more complex spread.

It may be helpful when undertaking a Tarot reading session to start with one of the simple spreads, and then to do one such as this 21-Card Spread; thus, information gained in the simple spread can be elaborated upon in the more complex one. For instance, if the session had begun

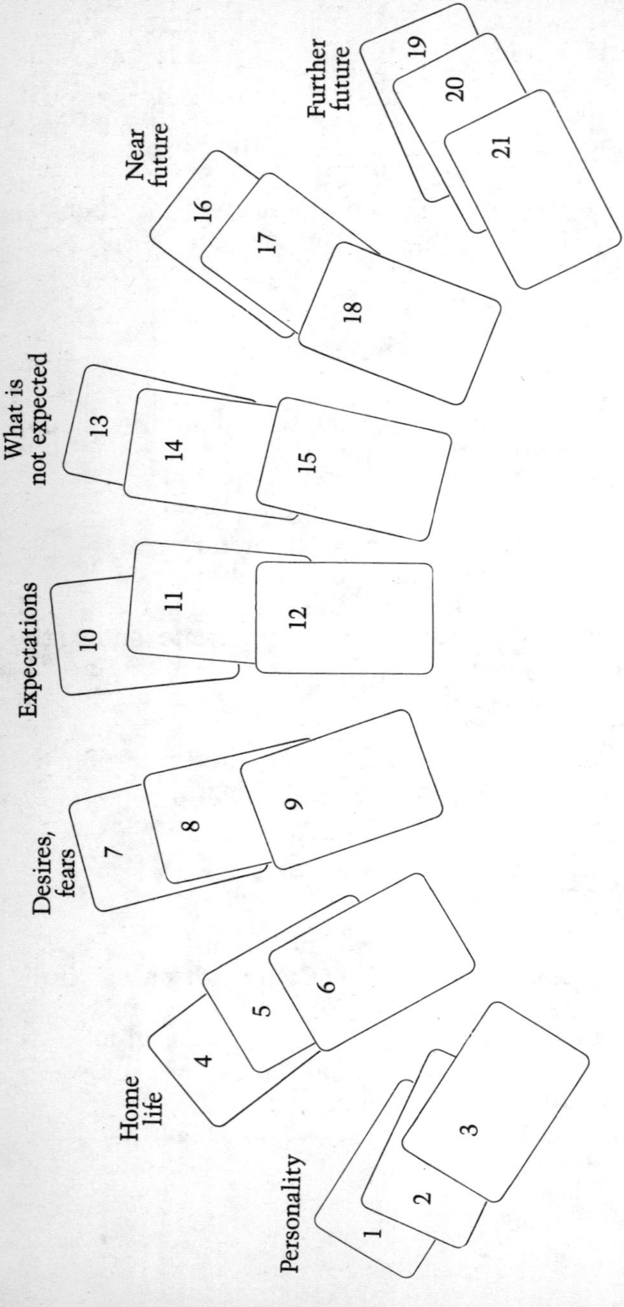

21-Card Spread

with the Nine-Card Spread described above, a card such as The Empress in position 5 would indicate a happy and secure home life and family relationships. Now, when following this up with the 21-Card Spread for the same Querent, the cards in positions 4, 5 and 6 will either confirm or seem to contradict that original impression. Suppose that this time, The Empress appears reversed in the position of 'Home life', accompanied by the Two of Swords and the Prince of Wands reversed. This may appear to contradict the message of the first spread and confuse the new student of Tarot but it should not automatically be assumed that the whole reading is now invalid or inaccurate. The Tarot reader's reaction should be to try to make sense of the cards as they happen to have turned up, finding meaning rather than nonsense, in the apparent contradiction. One possible interpretation, for instance, would be that the family situation or home life is generally secure and happy, but that some sort of trouble (probably temporary) has recently been provoked by someone displaying the unpredictable and disruptive qualities associated with the reverse aspect of the Prince of Wands.

The combination of cards in this spread could lead to a number of different interpretations. Sometimes in any group of three cards the individual cards will support one another, suggesting one distinct coherent picture. Sometimes, however, a group of three may contain cards with disparate or contradictory meanings. The reader should now use his intuition and imagination to suggest an interpretation that is not confusing or contradictory. Conflicting meanings between cards in any group of three would, for instance, point to an actual conflict in that area of the Querent's life. On the other hand, one or two cards in the group may show the normally prevailing situation, while a third, conflicting, card indicates new developments that have arisen or have been introduced into that situation.

As with the other spreads described earlier, cards in the positions of 'Expectations' and 'What is not expected' should be interpreted with reference to one another. As there are three cards in each position (10, 11 and 12, and 13, 14 and 15), it may be helpful to read 10 in conjunction with 13, 11 in conjunction with 14, and 12 in conjunction with 15. Likewise, it may be helpful to compare or contrast other adjacent cards, or cards in the same horizontal row (1, 7 and 10, for instance or 14 with 17).

With regard to the last six cards that represent the future, several problems may arise in interpreting them or in placing them on a time-scale. The cards numbered 16, 17 and 18 may be read together as representing one event in the near future, and, similarly, 19, 20 and 21 may be read together in this way to represent an event in the further future. Alternatively, each card may be seen as signifying an individual event, and the cards may be read in sequence, progressing into the future.

Accurately dating these future events is one of the most difficult aspects of Tarot reading. Some Tarot readers advocate certain rigid ways of calculating the dates according to the symbolism and numbering on the cards, but this approach tends to be confusing, and is out of keeping with the free and intuitive approach to interpreting the cards. Generally speaking, however, we can say that a reading is unlikely to predict very far into the future; it is more likely to apply to weeks and months rather than years. One good guide of the timing is the reader's own common sense when considering the events that appear to be predicted in the cards. It is usually the case that the Querent is concerned that certain present problems and queries should be resolved in a reading, and the Tarot reader would be wise to suppose that the spread is a coherent whole and that consequently the future events indicated are directly related to present situations and difficulties. Firstly, simply from knowing what the Querent's present situation is, common sense will often suggest a correct time-scale for the future events indicated. If, for instance, the Querent approaches the Tarot reader to ask for help in making an important decision which has to be made within the next few days, the reading will presumably be concerned with this problem, and is likely to show the unfolding of events within the next few days, as pertaining to that particular issue. On the other hand, should the Querent be concerned with more long-term prospects, the reading is likely to apply to a period extending some months into the future.

Secondly, a good guide to the time-scale is to consider cards that represent the past, and to assume that the reading extends into the future for the same time-span as it extends into the past. In the 21-Card Spread we are now considering, there is no position that specifically represents the past; however, cards in the positions of 'Personality.' or 'Home life' may relate to particular events that can be dated, and this would provide the necessary clues. Furthermore, if this spread is being done as a follow-up to a simpler spread which did show past events (such as The Celtic Cross), the dating of the events shown in the earlier spread can be used as a guide for putting a suitable time-scale on this second spread.

Again, there are no hard and fast rules here. Reading the cards is a skill that is acquired through experience, and the student should feel free to give an individual and creative interpretation, using intuition and common sense. Some people find that they are able to do this quite easily, approaching the cards with confidence and an open mind from the start. Others, however, have the wrong approach, viewing the cards with a superstitious and fearful attitude that leads to inhibited and foolish interpretations of a spread. For instance, it is absurd to suppose that the cards are predicting disasters and bizarre strokes of fate which are unrelated to present events or to what actual people involved in the situation are doing or intending to do. If, for example, a breakdown in a relationship is indicated in the cards, this must be the result of thoughts and actions of the participants in that relationship and not some stroke of ill-luck which will descend upon the unfortunate victims regardless of anything they themselves do. The cards should be used to give advice and guidance and should not be seen as fatalistically predicting what is destined to be or what is outside the control of human agents.

It is generally advisable for the Tarot reader to regard his or her skills as an aid to the Querent's decision-making and as a means of clarifying the present situation, suggesting possible solutions or outcomes and helping to put the Querent's present concerns into perspective. The next spread we shall look at, therefore, is one that will be particularly helpful in deciding upon the best course of action when alternatives are available.

ALTERNATIVES SPREAD

This spread is intended to show what will happen if the Querent pursues a course of action he is already considering and also what would happen if he were not to do this or were to do something else instead.

The order in which the cards are laid out suggests the way in which they should be interpreted: 1 is laid opposite 2, 3 opposite 4 and 5 opposite 6. The cards can therefore be seen as pairs, the individual cards in each pair 'opposing' one another in a way that should make evident both the contrasts and the similarities in the two different situations. The cards at the top of the spread — 5, 1 and 3 — show what will be likely to happen if the Querent proceeds in the way he is presently considering; while 4, 2 and 6 show some, alternative.

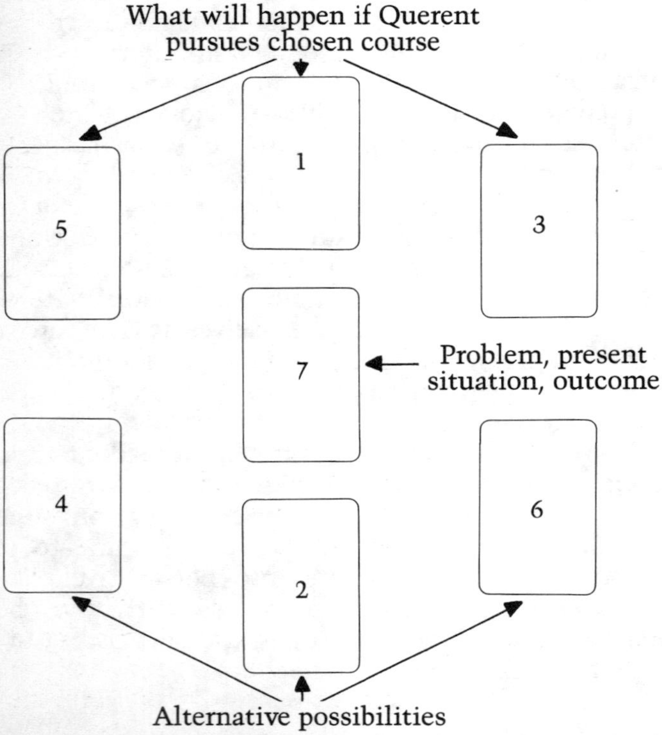

Alternative Courses of Action Spread

The alternative could be a number of things. It may suggest some better course of action that the Querent had not thought of; it may suggest some course of action which he had thought of but had decided to reject, and hopefully the reading would show whether he was wise or not in so doing; but often the alternative will simply show how the present problems which the Querent is experiencing will continue to be problems for him or will grow better of their own accord if he takes no active steps to improve matters.

Card number 7 should be interpreted in a similar way to 'The Outcome' position in the Celtic Cross Spread. It can show a possible solution, but is more likely to present a general view of the situation, clarifying a particular problem or pointing to some aspect of it which is important to consider.

This spread is useful if the Querent wants an answer to a specific question, such as 'Should I go abroad?', 'Should I change my job?', 'Should I leave my husband?' and so on. If the Querent has no such question in mind and is just confused about what to do, having no ideas about future courses of action, or if he merely wishes to know the likely outcome of some current matter, this spread would not be appropriate, and it would be better to use some other spread such as the Celtic Cross.

THE HOROSCOPE SPREAD AND THE TREE OF LIFE SPREAD

Finally we include two other spreads which give a general view ranging over different areas of the Querent's life.

The layout of the Horoscope Spread is based on the sequence of the astrological houses, each position being ascribed its meaning according to the attributes of the house that its position represents.

Again, it will be found that some of the positions in these spreads seem inappropriate to some readings. For instance, in the Horoscope Spread, card number 8, or 6, will not show anything relating to legalities, deaths or health, if these are not significant issues in the Querent's present circumstances; but nevertheless, the cards that appear in

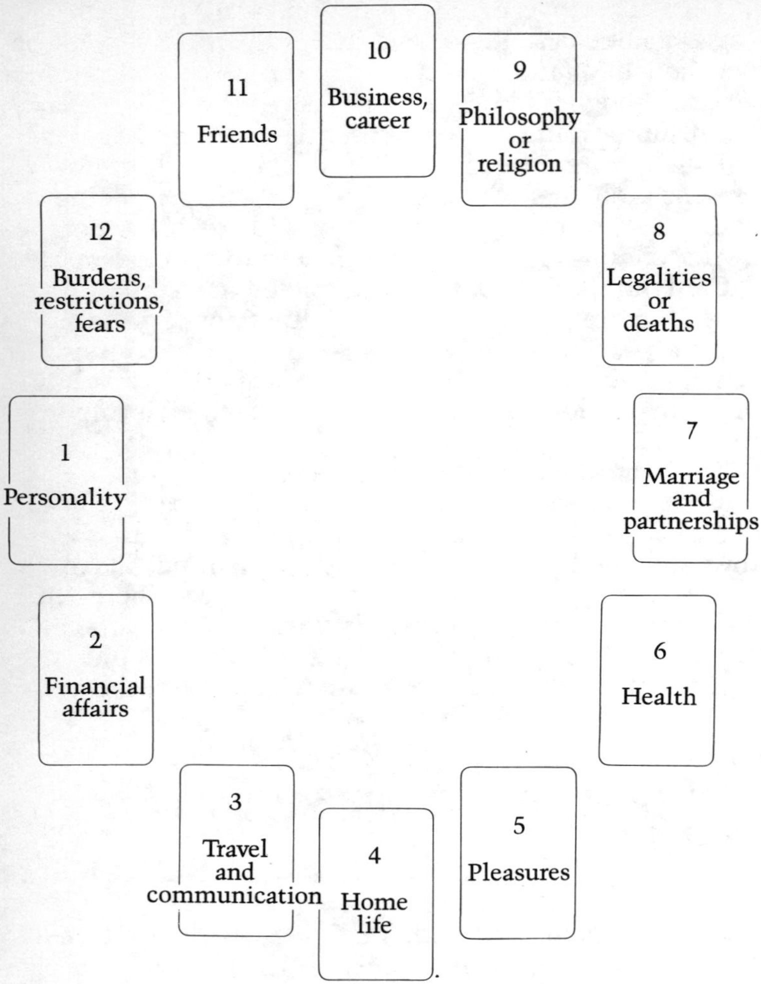

Horoscope Spread

these positions may supplement the information given in other areas of the spread. As always, the reader should be flexible and use intuition and common sense to find the best interpretation, seeing the layout as a guideline or framework to aid interpretation, and not as a rigid structure which may serve to impose entirely inappropriate meanings upon the reading.

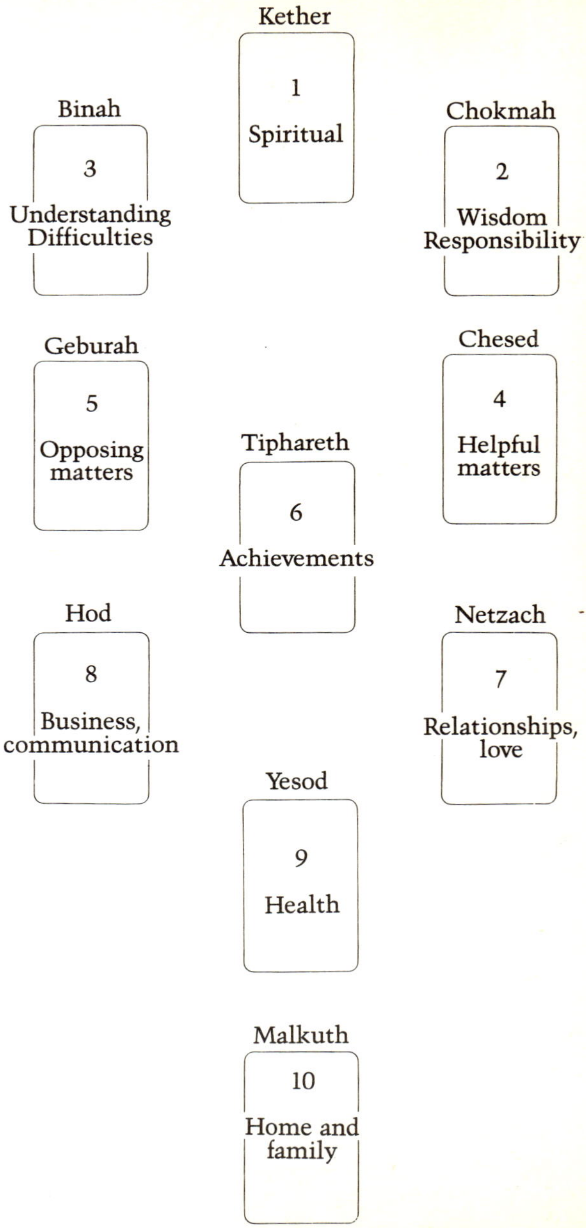

The Tree of Life Spread

CHAPTER FOUR
THE MAJOR ARCANA

O THE FOOL

Traditional Interpretation

The image on this card is sometimes of a court jester, sometimes of a ragged wanderer or beggar, sometimes a child or young person, often in brightly coloured clothing. This is the wise fool, someone who is outside normal society, in some sense free of the restrictions that convention imposes on most people, and who, because of this freedom, is able to gain insights denied to others. He is the innocent child who is uninhibited by self-consciousness, a sense of propriety, or the need to conform; he is the medieval court jester or fool who is given licence to make fun of the king and the royal court; he is the wanderer who has gained enlightenment by rejecting the conventional way of life. He embodies the ideas of innocence, love of life, enthusiasm and openness to future possibilities.

In a spread this card indicates opportunities, a new way of life, renewed energy, excitement and enthusiasm about new projects, and a carefree sense of well-being. It suggests any or all of these interpretations, depending upon its position in the spread. It is often said to represent an intuitive leap into the unknown. It can indicate the willingness to take a risk, or using intuition to make a difficult decision. There is a feeling of trust or faith that whatever happens will be for the best, and an ability, more often seen in children than in adults, to live in the present and enjoy one's present experience to the fullest without unnecessary worries about the future.

REVERSED

When the Fool appears reversed in a spread, the same innocent carefree qualities as described above are indicated, but now this attitude is inappropriate. Foolish decisions and reckless behaviour are likely, because no proper foresight has been taken. The Querent may feel restless and impatient; possibly he is reluctant to make commitments or to take responsibility, abandoning relationships and projects whenever problems arise. A desire to enjoy the pleasures of the moment leads to the avoidance of actions and situations that could lead to real or lasting happiness.

Interpretation for Relationships

This card can signify the start of a new relationship and the exhilaration of falling in love. A carefree, uninhibited attitude to love and sexual matters is indicated.

REVERSED

When reversed this card signifies a naïve or irresponsible attitude displayed by the Querent in his love life. Foolish infatuation, fickle relationships and ignorance or carelessness in sexual matters, are possible interpretations.

I THE MAGICIAN

Traditional Interpretation

Early Tarot decks show the Magician as a conjuror or juggler who performs with skill and dexterity, creating illusions to entertain an audience. Modern decks usually present him as a real magician trained in the magical arts, the four symbols of the Major Arcana (wand, cup, sword and disc) displayed as ritual instruments on the table before him. The Magician is the embodiment of certain aspects of the masculine principle; he is often depicted holding a rod which is a phallic symbol.

In its upright position, therefore, this card signifies confidence, intelligence and practical ability, which are regarded as extrovert or masculine qualities. It suggests not only the mental capacity and imagination to have ideas and to make plans, but also the ability to translate ideas into action; to channel one's mental energy into productive activities that lead to success in any area to which the agent applies himself. The card may represent a need to put ideas into practice or show that the time is right to do so if this is not already happening.

REVERSED

If The Magician is reversed, the creative energy is being inhibited or misused in some way. This will either be due to difficult circumstances or, more likely, because of the Querent's present attitude. The problem here could be that the Querent is using his skills selfishly or dishonestly, or it could be that he is lacking in confidence and determination, or is even afraid of success. The positive qualities that the Magician possesses are almost certainly present here, but it is a question of using this energy to the right ends and overcoming inhibitions and despondency.

Interpretation for Relationships

As a representation of the masculine principle, The Magician symbolizes masculine virility and sexual energy. Confidence and personal satisfaction in the Querent's love life are indicated when this card appears in a spread. It can also signify the channelling of sexual energy into productive, creative, artistic or spiritual activities and projects — the sublimation of sexual energy for a higher good.

REVERSED

Impotence and sexual frustration are indicated. The Querent may be putting a great deal of effort into an unsatisfying relationship which provides little in return, leaving him weak and lacking in confidence. Shyness and timidity in sexual matters is an alternative interpretation.

II THE HIGH PRIESTESS (OR THE PAPESS)

Traditional Interpretation

This card is known as The Papess (The Female Pope) in traditional decks, but in modern decks it is usually called The High Priestess. The title suggests an heretical notion which combines the ideas of religious institutions and teaching with femininity, folk legend and the flouting of laws and conventions. It is assumed to be an allusion to the story that one of the popes was in fact a woman in disguise.

The card is associated with the virgin aspect of the feminine principle. Some interpreters, emphasizing the

virginity of The High Priestess, have seen the opening between the two pillars in front of which the figure sits as a symbol of the vagina, while the curtain which hangs between the pillars may be seen as the unperforated hymen.

This card signifies guidance or instruction, particularly of a spiritual or moral nature, which comes from a mysterious or unconventional source — often from the Querent's own unconscious mind. The 'feminine' concepts represented here are 'inner' as opposed to 'outer', 'darkness' as opposed to 'light', 'unconscious' as opposed to 'conscious', 'intuition' as opposed to 'reason', and so on — all ideas which suggest guidance from the inner self, from dreams and from feelings of intuition. The message of this card is to listen to that quiet inner voice, to follow one's feelings, to do what one inwardly knows is right, rather than take the path of plain reason.

This card can also indicate unrealized inner potential and possibly occult powers or influences.

REVERSED

Intuitions, feelings and ideas are being ignored or suppressed. The Querent may have gifts and talents which are not being exercised, or there is a general failure to recognize one's real inner needs and feelings. If this card appears reversed it may be an explanation for other negative features in the spread, since someone who is out of touch with their unconscious or inner self can experience all kinds of difficulties, from trouble in relationships and minor practical problems, right through to a sense of apathy, worthlessness or despair. The reverse aspects of this card emphasize the importance of taking heed of one's real needs and feelings.

Interpretation for Relationships

Traditionally this card has been associated with the virgin aspect of the feminine principle. It can represent virginity or chastity, but may also signify initiation into sexual secrets. In a male Querent's spread it may represent his anima — the feminine aspect of his own personality — showing the need to allow the expression of this part of himself.

REVERSED
When reversed, this card indicates insensitivity in relationships; a denial of affection and of one's sexual and emotional needs. In a male Querent's spread it can represent the denial of the feminine side of his nature.

III THE EMPRESS

Traditional Interpretation

Like The High Priestess, this card symbolizes aspects of the feminine principle. The Empress represents Nature in all her bounty. She is a warm, welcoming environment, a comfortable home, good relationships, sensuality, love, enjoyment of life, marriage, sexuality, childbirth and motherhood. She represents both physical and emotional security and a strong sense of well-being and fulfilment which leads to generosity, a kindly outlook, the enjoyment of company, and a readiness to help others.

REVERSED
When this card appears reversed in a spread, it frequently indicates domestic problems. More generally it shows a sense of being ill at ease in the world. This feeling may arise because of adverse material circumstances, problems in personal relationships, arguments with friends or family, loneliness for whatever reason, and illness or poverty. Emotional insecurity is indicated, which may be a direct result of upheavals, major changes and disappointments.

Interpretation for Relationships

Sensuality and sexual well-being are shown here. The Querent has a secure relationship, gives and receives love and affection, and enjoys sensual pleasures. Pregnancy may be indicated. This is a card of good fortune with regard to all sexual matters.

REVERSED
Sexual problems may be represented by the reverse aspect of The Empress. It could signify an unfulfilling or exploitative relationship, sex without love, or problems in pregnancy. Unwanted pregnancy, miscarriage or infertility may be indicated.

IV THE EMPEROR

Traditional Interpretation

This card depicts a stern, rather forbidding figure, which represents certain characteristics of the masculine

principle. As opposed to the 'feminine' concepts of 'inner', 'unconscious', 'domesticity', 'emotion', and so on, the 'masculine' concepts embodied by the Emperor are 'outer', 'conscious', 'reason', 'order' and 'will'. He is frequently depicted holding a sceptre and orb, which are ancient sexual symbols: the orb is a female symbol, the sceptre a male symbol. Traditionally, royalty carried these objects as a sign that both the masculine and feminine principles were united in them personally, endowing the royal personage with divine or magical power.

The Emperor represents earthly power and authority, and the institutions of society. When this card appears in a spread it often indicates that the Querent himself has a mature, rational outlook and holds a responsible position that carries respect and authority. It can therefore also signify promotion or some outward form of recognition of these rational, organizational qualities. Sometimes, however, it suggests that authority, rules, and regulations have an important influence upon the Querent's life, either through the influence of particular people known to the Querent, or because of present circumstances, including a career or way of life which calls for a high degree of order and regulation.

REVERSED

There are problems in coming to terms with authority and

convention. The Querent may find himself in a position which he resents because he is made to feel inferior or irresponsible. This can mean that the present situation does not allow him sufficient scope to exercise his real capacity. On the other hand, the card can show someone who has never properly grown up and who is therefore unable or unwilling to take on responsibility. The reason for this could lie in childhood difficulties, the influence of a domineering parent, or of someone who even now is attempting to confine the Querent within a dependent, childlike role.

Interpretation for Relationships

Even in its upright position this is not a particularly auspicious card with regard to personal relationships. It may indicate an over-reliance on convention and on outward forms and appearances, and a difficulty in expressing genuine feelings. When the Querent is male, this card may suggest that he is concerned with his own sexual prowess and virility at the expense of showing affection for his partner. In a woman's spread it may represent a man in her life who is inclined to display a rather male chauvinist attitude.

REVERSED
A close relationship has deteriorated into one of domination and submission. The emotional atmosphere is one of coldness and selfishness. In its extreme form the reverse aspect of this card could indicate a sado-masochistic relationship.

V THE HIGH PRIEST (OR THE HEIROPHANT/THE POPE)

Traditional Interpretation

As one would expect, traditionally this card signified religious guidance and the teaching of the Church. Although it may still carry this meaning in a particular reading, since we now live in a largely secular society in

which most people are no longer strongly influenced by the Church, the card is more likely to signify guidance or teaching from some other source. Like the Church, however, this other source of information is likely to be some institution, professional body or person offering such a service, rather than a personal friend or family member.

If The High Priest appears in a spread, it may indicate that the Querent is a teacher or student in a school, college or university. It may, however, represent the need to seek information or advice with regard to a specific problem. A visit to a doctor, solicitor, personal counsellor, marriage guidance bureau, and so on, are all possible interpretations of this card.

REVERSED

The idea of teaching, learning or seeking advice is also contained in the reverse meaning of the card, but there may be a warning here — perhaps conventional, orthodox solutions to a current problem will be ineffectual; there may be a danger of being misled by bad advice. In some circumstances The High Priest reversed can represent at one and the same time both a difficult problem and good advice which will help to solve that problem. However, it is likely to indicate that going through conventional channels or seeking professional advice is not the ideal solution, and that being self-reliant and using one's own initiative on this occasion may bring more satisfactory results.

Interpretation for Relationships

The Querent may be seeking help and advice with regard to a close personal relationship. A visit to the doctor about a sexual matter, or a visit to a marriage guidance counsellor are possible interpretations.

REVERSED
Someone may be giving the Querent unhelpful or bad advice about his relationships or sexual problems under the guise of professional counselling. This advice is detrimental and he would do best to disregard it.

VI THE LOVERS

Traditional Interpretation

Older versions of this card often depict a young man standing between two women while Eros hovers above them, an arrow poised on his drawn bowstring. Modern versions usually show the young man with only one woman, and substitute an angel for Eros. The Rider-Waite version depicts a naked man and woman standing before the Tree of Life and the Tree of Knowledge, like Adam and Eve before the Fall. Other versions of the card are variously thought to represent the Judgement of Paris, a marriage ceremony, or a young couple finding true love. The Norse Tarot depicts the temptation of the goddess Freya to be unfaithful to her husband by having sex with the dwarf in return for the gift of a necklace: she has difficulty in choosing whether to remain faithful or not.

The card may be interpreted as signifying love or marriage. A more general interpretation of the card plays down the 'love' aspect; any difficult decision may be represented here, concerning career or any other matter in the Querent's life. The important element is that the situation is one in which two or more possible courses of action are open to him and any decision, once made, is probably irreversible and will require significant changes in the Querent's lifestyle. The choice should not be made lightly; careful thought and consideration is necessary, but if the card is upright it indicates that the best choice will eventually be made.

REVERSED

There is a danger of making an ill-considered decision which will later be regretted. Alternatively the Querent may be reluctant to make an important decision because he does not want to take responsibility for his own actions, and hopes instead to maintain a situation as it has been in the past. In either case a timid, immature attitude and a tendency to rely too much upon other people or to meekly follow the path of least resistance is probably the underlying problem here. There is a need to think more carefully about one's own direction and aims in life, and to start making proper plans for the future.

Interpretation for Relationships

Commitment to a long-term relationship is indicated; engagement or marriage may be imminent. The Querent has to make an important decision about his current relationship — whether to commit himself more deeply than before or whether to leave this person. The decision is likely to bring about a radical change in circumstances, and once the choice has been made it will be very hard, if not impossible, to turn back. Traditionally the card has sometimes been seen as representing the Querent's choice between two prospective partners — in accepting one he has to reject the other and he cannot go back on his decision once it is made.

REVERSED
When this card appears reversed, the Querent should take particular care about any important decisions concerning his love life. It may indicate, for instance, that the decision to end a relationship would not be a good one, or that the full implications have not been thought through. Alternatively it may indicate that a prospective match would be unwise.

VII THE CHARIOT

Traditional Interpretation

The traditional picture shows a man in armour standing in a chariot which is drawn by two horses or sphinxes, usually one of which is black and the other white. In the Norse Tarot, these animals are goats. The image is thought to represent a victorious warrior; it suggests courage and skill which lead to success and triumph over obstacles and adversities. The white and black horses or sphinxes are said to represent opposing forces in the charioteer's life, or opposing elements of his own psyche, which are tamed and controlled by the strength of his will alone. The Rider-Waite version of this card shows the emblem of the *lingam* and *yoni* (symbols of the penis and vagina) emblazoned on an escutcheon on the front of the chariot, signifying the harmonious union of the masculine and feminine principles. The card represents courage, will-power and ambition, and all the qualities of organization and determination which will lead to success and high achievement. The martial imagery here indicates that there will be struggle and conflict too, however. This may either arise from external circumstances, or will be an inner, psychological conflict between desires or impulses. Great self-control and strength of will, and a clear sense of purpose and direction are indicated.

REVERSED
The strength and ambition associated with the upright meaning of the card is misdirected when it is reversed. This leads to feelings of restless confusion and a lack of any clear sense of direction or purpose. Ambition turns to anger and frustration, and strength of will becomes aggressive self-assertion which overrides reason and consideration for the feelings of others. A very trying situation, difficult obstacles and big changes in one's life may be the root cause of these negative feelings and attitudes. Possibly the Querent is trying to tackle a problem that is too big for him, or is motivated by feelings of resentment or a desire for revenge, but his approach is perhaps the wrong one.

Interpretation for Relationships

With regard to personal relationships, this is not a good card. It suggests that the Querent may be selfish or over-demanding in the relationship, trying to impose his will upon his partner. It may also indicate conflicting desires or passions, or the Querent's sexual or emotional impulses being at odds with his reason. A calmer, slower approach is called for, with more consideration for the needs of others.

REVERSED
Sexual frustration is indicated. The Querent may feel that his relationships are fumbling and blundering or that he is taking the wrong course or making the wrong approach altogether. A reassessment of the situation is necessary in order for the Querent to decide what he really wants from his personal relationships and whether or not his present approach is appropriate.

VIII JUSTICE

Traditional Interpretation

This card usually depicts the conventional personification of Justice as a woman bearing balanced scales and a sword. The sword and scales may be seen as sexual symbolism. The sword symbolizes an erect phallus, and the scales represent testicles. This is particularly noticeable in Aleister Crowley's version of the card, and he refers to Justice as The Woman Satisfied, implying sexual satisfaction. In the Norse Tarot, the figure is male and represents Forseti, law-giver to the Norse gods. In a spread it represents justice, a fair outcome, rational judgement, arbitration, balance and freedom from bias. It can represent an actual court case or an encounter with the law. More generally it signifies that justice will prevail. Where judgements or decisions are to be made, they will be made fairly; disagreements will be resolved in a fair and rational manner, possibly with the assistance of some third party acting as an arbitrator. In a previously confusing or chaotic situation, order and balance will be restored.

REVERSED
Injustice and imbalance is signified here and the Querent may be the victim of this — perhaps he feels that he has been treated unfairly. If the card represents a court case or legal matter, the implication is that the outcome will go against him. On the other hand, if he is in the wrong himself, the reverse aspect of this card may indicate that he will suffer as a consequence of justice being done; the balance will be righted and he will have to pay for his past misdemeanours.

Interpretation for Relationships

The Querent is concerned about fairness and equality in his relationships. This card may appear in a spread if the Querent feels that at present he is being treated unfairly. Sometimes it appears when a relationship has already broken down and the Querent has had to resort to legal arbitration. When the card is upright, the outcome appears favourable.

REVERSED
The Querent feels he is being treated unfairly in his relationship and that his partner is unable or unwilling to see his point of view. In extreme cases unpleasant legal proceedings may be indicated.

IX THE HERMIT

Traditional Interpretation

A hermit is a person who has left society, avoiding the distractions and preoccupations of social interaction and concern for material things, in order to turn his attention inwards upon spiritual values and personal development. The card therefore represents a need to withdraw from a situation in order to think quietly by oneself. It may be a

time of decision or reassessment of oneself, one's life and one's values; or perhaps there is a need for rest and recovery after a period of hard work and activity.

The message here may be that the answer to a current problem lies within, in the Querent's own attitudes and decisions. Only he can discover what his real feelings and needs are, and only he can decide the course that his life should take. Help from other people is either not available at this time or should not be relied upon too heavily. The final answers lie with the Querent himself.

REVERSED

Obstinate self-reliance becomes a problem when the card is reversed. The Querent is struggling with difficulties alone when help is needed; possibly he is declining help that has been offered. Isolation, loneliness and self-pity are indicated. Possibly the Querent is resisting change, clinging to the past and resenting any attempts by others to persuade him to adapt or to co-operate with them. He may even be acting against his own better judgement in this. The advice here must be to adopt a more open-minded attitude and to accept change as a necessary part of life.

Interpretation for Relationships

The Querent needs space for himself within his relationship. This card may indicate that he has spent too much time on the needs of his partner and it is now time to think of his own needs as well. This may include speaking to his partner about his sexual needs which he has denied until now.

Alternatively the card may show that the Querent is reluctant to engage in a relationship at this time, preferring independence. Cessation of sexual activity and the need to withdraw from sexual relationships temporarily may be indicated.

REVERSED
The Querent desires a close relationship but does not have one at this time. Loneliness and isolation are indicated. The Querent may feel that he has been rejected and that nobody loves him. The reverse aspects of this card may represent enforced celibacy, or divorce, or widowhood, leaving the Querent without a sexual partner.

X THE WHEEL OF FORTUNE

Traditional Interpretation

This card signifies the apparent chance workings of fate or luck, and its implications in the Querent's life. Good or ill luck seems to occur at random and everyone has their share of both. When the card is upright it indicates that there will be changes for the better. What seem to be chance occurrences will bring opportunities and important developments into the Querent's life. Past difficulties and struggles will come to an end and a period of success and good fortune will follow.

From a different viewpoint, however, these apparently inexplicable happenings can be seen as fate and fulfilment of destiny.

REVERSED

The reverse aspects of this card signify a turn for the worse. The Querent may suffer misfortunes that appear to come out of the blue. Again, as with the upright meaning of the card, unforeseen events and changes may seem to happen for no reason and appear to be simply a matter of chance and random factors operating. If there is some reason or ordering behind such events, then its true nature is usually beyond the grasp of human comprehension.

Interpretation for Relationships

A chance occurrence may lead to the development of a new relationship. A change of fortune for the better in the Querent's love life is indicated.

REVERSED

A deterioration in a personal relationship is suggested. Hopes and expectations with regard to a relationship are unlikely to be fulfilled at present. The Querent may be in for a disappointment.

XI STRENGTH (OR FORTITUDE)

Traditional Interpretation

The most common image on this card is of a woman taming a lion, its jaws held firmly in her hands. In the Norse Tarot, the picture shows the sky god Tyr binding the monstrous wolf Fenris. Other versions depict Hercules wrestling with the Nemean Lion, which also conveys the idea of great physical strength. It is moral strength, courage and the

strength

power of conviction that is emphasized in this card, however.

The lion or wolf can be seen as some aspect of the Querent which at first sight seems dangerous, destructive and uncontrollable, but which can become a source of personal strength when confronted and its energy properly utilized. Powerful emotions and desires, in particular those which may be thought of as base or evil (such as anger or sexual desire) become all the greater when they are suppressed and denied; the energy they contain, having no other outlet, can cause anxiety, depression, and even physical symptoms. It is such feelings that the wild beast represents. By running away from them they become wild, frightening and monstrous; but by recognizing and confronting them, it becomes possible to use that energy for positive ends, and so what appeared to be a wild beast is tamed to become a source of inner strength. When the card appears upright, it indicates that the Querent is able to draw upon this inner source of strength to tackle any matter in hand.

REVERSED

An obvious interpretation of the reverse aspects of this card is to say that it signifies weakness, but the precise nature of this weakness may be more difficult to define. As indicated above, what appears to be weakness or fear may in fact be a source of strength which has not been properly directed.

When this card appears reversed in a spread, it generally indicates that the Querent feels unable to cope with a certain task and lacks confidence in his own ability. The reason for this may be that he is attempting something that is really beyond his ability; but his doubts and fears and feelings of weakness may equally be illusions arising from his failure to recognize his own strengths. There may be a tendency here to use inner energy in worrying and self-condemnation, surrendering to fears and morbid fantasies, instead of directing that energy outwards to be used constructively in resolving problems.

Interpretation for Relationships

This card can be seen as representing powerful sexual desires — indeed, Aleister Crowley renamed it Lust. These sexual desires must be channelled in the right direction and be given a legitimate outlet. Used in a positive way they can be a source of strength and energy to the Querent.

REVERSED

Sexual guilt and suppressed sexual feelings are indicated when this card is reversed. Harm may result if the Querent persists in denying these natural inclinations, and sexuality can become a dangerous, destructive drive if it is not acknowledged and given expression.

XII THE HANGED MAN

Traditional Interpretation

The picture on this card is certainly one of the strangest in the entire Tarot deck, and its meaning at first sight is not at all clear. Some decks unfortunately depict the man as dead or unconscious, his head lolling on the ground, which carries disturbing and ominous connotations. In fact, the upright meaning of the card is very positive. It has been suggested by some commentators that the image alludes to the ritual sacrifice of Odin upon the Tree of Life in order to attain enlightenment, and indeed this is the scene depicted in the Norse Tarot version of the card. Some decks show the

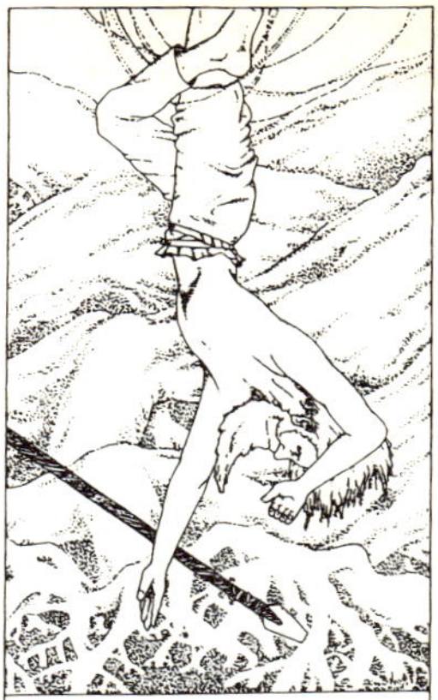

the hanged man

figure's head haloed, his face tranquil, portraying acceptance and mystical understanding.

The meaning of this card when upright is that the Querent will be able to realize his full potential in dedicating himself to some major personal project. It is important here that though what the Querent does may appear foolish and odd to other people, it is of the greatest value to him. The upside-down position of the man in the picture represents the Querent's own altered or unusual viewpoint, which may be hard for others to understand. A personal experience of great value is signified here, but it may involve making sacrifices which other people consider unacceptable, though the Querent expects to gain more in other respects than he is losing. It frequently signifies sacrifice of material comforts and the abandonment of an egotistical outlook in order to make important personal, idealistic or spiritual gains.

REVERSED

When reversed, this card indicates a deep unease and dissatisfaction with oneself and one's life. The Querent is denying an important part of himself and feels unable to commit himself very strongly to anything. As a result he may feel depressed and apathetic, seeing his life as futile, or being unable to find any satisfaction in apparent achievements.

It is likely that he is trying to act in accordance with other people's requirements and demands upon him, compromising his own values and repressing his own feelings out of a sense of duty or a desire to conform to society's expectations. A misplaced sense of value, a materialistic attitude, and feelings of being at odds with oneself and the world at large are all indicated here.

This card should be seen as a warning that the Querent needs to think about making changes in his life-style and attitudes, as this kind of destructive denial of one's own inner needs cannot be continued for long without unpleasant consequences.

Interpretation for Relationships

The Querent feels the need to dedicate himself to one special, deep relationship. His attitude is idealistic and highly romantic and he feels ready to sacrifice everything for love. To others he may appear rash and unrealistic, but his love is genuine and very strong. He is not interested in casual sexual dalliance, but wants to commit himself to a serious, long-term relationship. Alternatively the card may represent commitment to a sexual life-style or relationship of which other people disapprove.

REVERSED
The Querent is disillusioned with his relationship, but may be hiding his real feelings for the sake of appearances. He may have to face the possibility that his needs are different from what he once thought they were, and he may be searching for different qualities in a partner. Sexually ambivalent feelings and confusion over one's sexual identity may be indicated.

XIII DEATH

Traditional Interpretation

Sometimes people are frightened by this card because they imagine it means physical death. Only very rarely does it signify an actual death, and it never predicts the death of the

Querent himself. Instead it represents major changes in the Querent's life, showing that situations and patterns of behaviour that have continued until now will have to come to an end. Usually the Querent knows what these changes are and is already experiencing them. When the card is upright, this suggests that the change is accepted as necessary, or is even welcomed as a means of separating from an unpleasant past and moving on to new and better experiences. The kind of important changes that are indicated here, however, may bring some anxiety and sense of loss, because of their far-reaching effects and the impossibility of ever returning to what went before. Marriage, divorce, moving home, leaving school, starting a new job, or otherwise adopting a new way of life, can all be represented by this card.

The experience may be difficult, painful or disturbing in many ways, but it is also inevitable and is likely to make way for new opportunities in the future.

REVERSED

The kind of radical change described above is experienced as painful and destructive when this card appears reversed in a spread. It often indicates that change has been resisted and postponed, but in the end has come about from necessity, in spite of the Querent's attempts to prevent it. Continued resistance and struggle will cause more distress and will only delay developments which are inevitable. Difficulties which have been ignored may have become greater problems which now have to be confronted. Changes which should have been made voluntarily must now happen perforce, and may as a consequence be more difficult to handle.

Interpretation for Relationships

A radical change in the Querent's relationships can be represented by this card. It may indicate the ending of a relationship; but it can also show the start of a new relationship which will require a big change in the Querent's life. The experiences represented by this card are likely to be painful and emotionally disturbing, but these changes are necessary in order that something new and better may follow. The card can be seen as representing the end of sexual innocence or the loss of virginity.

REVERSED
The Querent may be struggling on with an unsatisfactory relationship or a persistent problem within his relationship and changes should have been made before now. It is time to recognize that some relationships can never be improved for the better. If the Querent is thinking of ending a relationship, this card indicates that it is high time he did; further delays will only cause more pain in the long run.

XIV TEMPERANCE

Traditional Interpretation

The word 'temperance' is often used to mean moderation and control of natural impulses which would lead to foolhardy behaviour. The meaning of 'temperance' in this card, however, is that of combination and the mixing of elements or qualities in the right proportions. The result of such a combination is balance and harmony. The traditional image on this card is of an angel pouring liquid from one vessel into another. Often one of the vessels is silver and the other gold, representing the moon and the sun — in other words, the feminine and masculine principles. The angel

temperance

combines the qualities of these two principles to produce a balanced and harmonious whole. The angel itself is a spiritual being that transcends sexuality, possessing both masculine and feminine attributes combined within its spiritual nature.

A person who practises temperance in this sense may appear self-controlled, calm and restrained in difficult circumstances, but the important feature here is balance. Nothing is repressed or held back to cause tension or inner turmoil. The temperate person is calmly capable, able to reconcile opposing desires and forces within himself to maintain composure without weakness or indecision.

When this card appears in a spread, it shows that the Querent is an efficient, responsible person who is able to cope in a situation where caution, tact and perseverance are required. Time should be taken to weigh up a problem carefully before acting; intuition and common sense will show the Querent what to do when the time comes.

REVERSED

Imbalance and conflict are the reverse aspects of this card. Moodiness and indecision are indicated, as the Querent wavers from one extreme to the other. He may be clumsy and blundering, making a mess of favourable situations, acting on impulse, blurting out thoughts and feelings that he will later regret, but holding back when something important needs to be said or done.

Inappropriate behaviour like this may be due to youth or inexperience, or perhaps simply to inexperience in one particular area or with regard to a specific issue. Sometimes it can represent feelings of restlessness, or fear of incompetence, rather than failure to cope in actual practice.

Interpretation for Relationships

If the Querent employs tact and caution in his love life, a harmonious relationship is possible. The card suggests that it is necessary to make a special effort to understand his partner's point of view. Finding this balance between their different needs and desires is important here. The Querent should recognize that quality of sexual experience is more important than quantity. Discretion and self-restraint are called for, as is mutual respect between partners.

REVERSED

Irrational passions and excessive behaviour are represented by the reverse aspect of this card. The Querent may be making unrealistic and inconsiderate sexual demands. The clumsy handling of personal relationships is indicated here.

XV THE DEVIL

Traditional Interpretation

Because of conventional notions about the Devil, this card is often seen as extremely sinister, representing evil, black magic, lust and temptation. This, however, is an extreme interpretation that is unlikely to apply in an ordinary Tarot reading, and trying to interpret it in this way can create absurd distortions in a reading.

This card, therefore, usually represents an oppressive, stifling influence in the Querent's life which creates tension, fear and anger which has no outlet. It indicates growing resentment and frustration with a situation in which one feels trapped and helpless. This concept of bondage and being trapped in a hopeless situation is very clearly portrayed in the Norse Tarot version of the card. In traditional versions of the card two small chained figures in the foreground of the picture show the Querent's own position, while the large, glowering, looming figure of the Devil behind them represents the oppressive problem which the Querent feels is bearing down on him and is the plague of his life.

When this card appears upright, it suggests that the Querent is attempting to live with the problem at present, and sees no way of escaping or making changes for the better. In particularly bad cases, perhaps this pessimistic outlook is justified, but with a mental burden as bad as this, the Querent should really be asking what is to be done to improve matters. Some solution may have been overlooked or rejected which would in fact be helpful. Other cards in the spread may suggest what this is.

REVERSED

The oppressive situation described above is probably long-standing when the card is reversed, and the Querent may have reached breaking point. The time has come to recognize that something must be done to lighten the burden and it is likely that some steps have already been taken to bring this about. The Querent probably admits to having reached the end of his tether, and is likely to be considering some course of action to alleviate present problems which have become intolerable.

Interpretation for Relationships

The Devil has always been associated with negative aspects of sexuality which arouse feelings of fear and disgust. The image on this card often presents the Devil as hermaphrodite, with prominent female breasts and conspicuous male genitalia. The overall impression is of a powerful force of sexuality which has become perverted towards evil ends. This card may represent an overwhelming sex drive, sexual domination or violence, sadism, adultery or perversion. The Querent is probably the victim of this oppression rather than the perpetrator.

REVERSED
When the card is reversed, it signifies much the same as the upright meaning, except that the circumstances are likely to have persisted for longer. The time has come for the Querent to find a way out of an oppressive and intimidating situation where sex, instead of being an expression of love, is used as a weapon.

XVI THE TOWER

Traditional Interpretation

The picture on this card is a violent image of destruction,

and, as might be expected, the meaning attached to it, even in its upright position, is that of disaster and bad fortune. The Tower may be seen as a gigantic, rigid phallic symbol which seemed indestructible yet has been struck down by natural forces outside human control. The destruction of certain facets of the masculine principle is symbolized; the downfall of the ego, the overthrow of rationality and a blow to the pride are all signified.

When the card appears in a spread, it indicates some traumatic experience for the Querent which usually occurs quite unexpectedly. This could be a physical accident, or it might equally well be a discovery or sudden revelation which comes as a terrible shock and causes great distress and emotional pain.

It should be noted, however, that though the experience may be seen as devastating at the time and may be viewed in an entirely negative light, in retrospect it will probably be seen as valuable. Such bolts from the blue can be seen as a test of one's strength and character, and what comes as a shattering blow can later be seen as a timely warning to make one stop, reconsider, and take a different view of oneself and one's aims. The Tower can represent a disturbing incident which has a sobering, humbling effect upon the Querent, particularly in the case of someone who previously had an inflated or unrealistic image of himself and his projects. Disillusionment of this kind, though crushing at the time, can have important and positive consequences in the long-term.

REVERSED

The unpleasant aspects of this card still remain when it is reversed, though their effect may be less devastating. Rather than a sudden unexpected, shattering blow, the misfortunes signified by The Tower reversed are likely to be of such a nature that they could have been foreseen and possibly avoided. The suggestion here is of disappointments and anti-climax when hopes fail to be realized, or when some long-awaited event does not live up to expectations. The positive attributes of the upright meaning of this card are unlikely to be present, however, apart from the fact that one usually learns from experience not to make the same mistakes again.

Interpretation for Relationships

The Querent receives a shock with regard to his love life. He may learn something disturbing about his partner which he did not know before and which causes him to see his partner in a new light. On the other hand, he or his partner may have an accident or health problem which disrupts their sex life. Shocking revelations, rows or physical injuries may be indicated. Sexual humiliation and embarrassing incidents are also possibities.

REVERSED
Problems in a relationship which could have been avoided now come to crisis point. Careless or unthoughtful behaviour in the past now brings unpleasant consequences. A relationship fails to live up to the Querent's expectations.

XVII THE STAR

Traditional Interpretation

In complete contrast to the previous card, The Star depicts a scene of great peace and tranquillity. The traditional image is of a naked young woman pouring water from two vessels at the edge of a still blue pool. The picture immediately suggests cleansing, refreshment and renewal. The two vessels may be seen as breasts, nourishing the psyche with spiritual milk.

The appearance of this card in a spread signifies hope, and the opportunity to recover after a period of struggle, hardship, or illness. There is rest, inspiration and the widening of horizons. The card can represent unexpected blessings and the relief from problems which may previously have seemed insoluble. It suggests an inner sense of calm, happiness, contentment and optimism. It can signify a return to health after physical illness.

REVERSED
When The Star appears reversed in a spread, this does not negate the good qualities associated with this card, but it suggests obstacles to happiness, and a tendency towards pessimism, even when circumstances are favourable. The Querent may lack self-confidence, feel afraid of the unknown and be unsure of himself, which can lead to a timid, nervous approach to life, and a reluctance to take chances or to see opportunities when they arise. Even when reversed, this card is a symbol of joy and hope; but the problem may be that the Querent has difficulty in appreciating this, because of an underlying insecurity.

Interpretation for Relationships

An improvement in the Querent's love life is indicated and there may be a widening of horizons to meet different people and possibly find a new sexual partner. Renewal of sexual energy and renewed enthusiasm in the Querent's relationship is signified. If the Querent has suffered in the relationship in the past, the situation will now improve, and peace, harmony and love will replace past problems.

REVERSED
The Querent is unable to fully appreciate the opportunities that are available to him. If he is looking for a new relationship, he may be missing an important opportunity. If he is already in a relationship, his pessimistic outlook and lack of enthusiasm are preventing him from enjoying the love that is offered him. Despite his negative outlook, the

situation is really very favourable. Love, tranquillity and sexual fulfilment are within his reach.

XVIII THE MOON

Traditional Interpretation

The traditional picture shows a bleak landscape with two dark towers in the distance and a dog and wolf howling at the full moon, while a large crayfish emerges from a pool in the foreground. The moon has a woman's face, usually in profile, representing the Moon Goddess, and accordingly this image can be seen as another aspect of the feminine principle that appeared in The High Priestess and The Empress. A close association between the moon and feminity has been observed from antiquity on account of women's menstrual cycle correlating with the phases of the moon. Some versions of the card personify the moon as a goddess. The Norse Tarot diverges from this tradition in having a male figure in the picture. The reason for this is that in Norse mythology the moon is personified as male, and the sun is personified as female, and in this respect it differs from the mythology of many other cultures.

The eeriness of the scene depicted on The Moon card and, in some versions, the lack of any human characters and the presence of non-human creatures, all help to convey an impression of something sinister, forbidding and alien.

When this card appears in a spread, the message is that the Querent, in some sense, must follow the path through this dim mysterious scene, alone and without any guide. Obviously, there are stong feelings of apprehension, doubt, loneliness and fear.

The card indicates that the Querent is facing some difficult problems with which he feels he must cope on his own. He may feel that he cannot see very far ahead and that there are unknown pitfalls awaiting him. The sense of the unknown and the unknowable, a lack of faith in one's own ability, and a tendency to imagine the worst, are very powerful here.

Bad dreams, morbid fantasies, depression, moodiness, insecurity, and sometimes gynaecological problems, may also be indicated when this card appears in a spread.

REVERSED
The fears and insecurity described above become a serious obstacle when The Moon appears reversed. The Querent feels unable to face the problems ahead; doubt and despair prevent any attempt at progress being made. The Querent may be unable to cope with this problem alone, and feels acutely the need for help and support, which will probably have to be found before any improvement can be made.

Interpretation for Relationships

This card can signify the lack of a close relationship in the Querent's life and the lack of sexual fulfilment. He feels isolated and without love. The fear associated with this card may be fear of sex, or a distaste for sexual activities. In a woman's spread, it can signify sexual inhibitions caused by physical problems; for example, some matter concerning menstruation or contraception may be important here. In a man's spread, it may signify fear or dislike of women.

REVERSED
Severe loneliness and depression are indicated when this card is reversed. The kind of problems associated with the upright meaning have probably persisted for longer if the card is reversed. Help and support from another person may be needed before any improvement can be made. If the

problem is of a medical nature the Querent should seek the advice of a doctor.

XIX THE SUN

Traditional Interpretation

As the moon has traditionally been seen as feminine and passive, associated with darkness and mystery, so the sun has been seen as masculine and active, the source of light and energy. Nevertheless, in one fifteenth-century deck (known as the Charles VI deck) the card of The Sun depicts a woman spinning; and, as already mentioned, in Norse mythology the sun was personified as female, which accounts for why a woman appears on this card in the Norse Tarot.

The usual image, however is of the bright face of the sun shining down upon two children in a garden; another common version shows a single child mounted on a horse. The picture conveys happiness, enjoyment, light-heartedness and a feeling of energy and vigour. The Sun is an obvious symbol of joy, optimism, high ideals, ambition and achievement.

When this card appears in a spread, it indicates success in any matter concerning the Querent. There is much power and confidence, contentment, and the ability to enjoy life to the full. Certainly The Sun is one of the most positive cards in the deck, and can only be a cause for concern if it appears in an otherwise negative spread, in which case it might indicate that the Querent is rather too ambitious and idealistic, or is setting his sights too high. In normal circumstances though, it can only represent the very best of joy and success.

REVERSED
The energy and optimism represented in this card is hard to suppress, even when reversed; the positive features here are very strong indeed. However, when the card is upside-down, it suggests some obstacle or difficulty in attaining happiness and success. It may be that the Querent feels dissatisfied or experiences a sense of anticlimax in spite of his achievements; while, on the other hand, he may have hopes and fantasies which are unrealistic and out of touch with what is possible at the present time. This could give rise to frustration and resentment, even when prospects look good and when there is still much to enjoy in the present. The Querent should not be too impatient or so easily discouraged but instead should take steps towards what is attainable at this time; greater hopes and ambitions can be realized later with steady effort, so long as the goal can be kept in view.

Interpretation for Relationships

This card stands for a contented and passionate relationship and complete sexual fulfilment. It is a most auspicious card for the Querent's love life, and signifies the attainment of his deepest desires.

REVERSED
The Querent is passionate and idealistic, but there are obstacles to the fulfilment of his desire. He may feel that his ideal partner is unattainable or that the relationship he already has is unsatisfactory. Wild sexual fantasies but a lack of real fulfilment may be indicated. Possibly the Querent is being unrealistic in his hopes, and the reality of his relationships never lives up to his dreams.

XX JUDGEMENT

Traditional Interpretation

The traditional version of this card depicts a typical resurrection scene, an angel blowing a trumpet while the dead rise from their graves. It symbolizes the end of one phase of life and the beginning of another, but also, importantly, there is the notion of judgement or assessment being applied at this point of change. The implication is that the Querent in some way judges or is judged; there is an assessment of his past life and of his own position in the present in respect of that.

When the card appears upright, it indicates that the Querent has come to the end of something, or is presently experiencing change of some sort, and that in looking back and assessing what has gone before he feels contentment, satisfaction and a sense of achievement. He may realize that past difficulties brought changes for the better, though this is a view he may not have had until now. Overall, he judges that what has happened is good and that his own actions were for the best.

REVERSED

The notions of judgement and the end of one stage of life and the beginning of the next still apply, but when the card is reversed, the judgement will be negative and accompanied by feelings of remorse. There will be regret for past actions, the thought that something should have been done that was left undone, or a feeling that one ought to have done more. It represents an unpleasant or unsatisfactory end to something, together with the Querent's feeling (which may or may not be justified) that the bad outcome could have been avoided.

Interpretation for Relationships

The Querent has reached a point where he needs to assess his past relationships and plan for the future. What appeared to be failures in the past can now be seen as developments that allowed changes for the better. The Querent is reconciled to his past actions and without regret accepts that everything has turned out for the best.

REVERSED
The Querent regrets past actions or events concerning a relationship or sexual activity, believing that matters would have turned out better if only he had behaved differently. Remorse about a broken love-affair or a failed marriage may be indicated. Shame over sexual misdemeanours can also be signified.

XXI THE WORLD

Traditional Interpretation

The traditional image on this card is rather different from the others in the Major Arcana in that there is no scene or landscape in which the figures are set. The various elements of the design are arranged upon a plain background. The central figure is usually a naked or semi-naked woman dancing; some commentators suggest that this figure is really hermaphrodite, symbolizing the perfect union of the masculine and feminine principles. The four creatures which appear in the corners in many versions of the card are regarded variously as symbols of the four elements, the four cardinal points, the four fixed signs of the zodiac, the four Evangelists or the Four Creatures of Ezekiel

The central dancing figure is often surrounded by a wreath of laurel leaves.

This card, as the final card in the Major Arcana, signifies completion and the successful outcome of any matter. It can represent the unity or wholeness of the self; the feeling of elation, well-being and a sense of oneness which is experienced at times of success and achievement and after surviving times of difficulty. This is a card of fulfilment, self-knowledge, release and freedom.

REVERSED

When the card is reversed, the success and completion it represents are hard to attain; there may be delays, frustrating obstacles and the wasting of energy in going over the same ground time and again. There is a sense here of being frustrated and trapped, usually because some matter which should have been completed is still dragging on, perhaps with little sign of a satisfactory outcome. The end may be within reach, if the Querent has the patience to wait and persevere for a while longer. On the other hand, if there is no indication of this, it may be a good time to make some attempt at breaking out of a vicious circle of events which shows no sign of being resolved and which has only become a burden and a drain upon the Querent's resources.

Interpretation for Relationships

This is a card of complete sexual and emotional fulfilment and liberation. Self-realization through a loving sexual relationship is indicated. The Querent may experience sex as a mystical union leading to enlightenment, for this card can be seen as representing sexual activity as a religious rite or sacrament, and sexuality used as a means to a higher end.

REVERSED

The reverse aspect of this card signifies boredom and stagnation in a relationship, or lack of variation in sexual activity. The Querent's love life is in a rut and he needs to make some changes in order to break out of a dull routine.

CHAPTER FIVE
THE COURT CARDS

The Court cards can be especially difficult to interpret as they may represent one of a number of different things, and there may be a problem in deciding which interpretation is the most appropriate.

Usually the Court cards are thought to represent particular individuals, either persons known to the Querent or with whom he or she will come into contact. They can also represent aspects of the Querent's own personality. However, it is not always possible to interpret these cards in this way, and on occasion it may seem more appropriate to interpret a Court card as representing some situation experienced by the Querent. This is more likely to be the case with the Princess and the Prince of each suit, and so for these cards we have supplied meanings which are applicable to situations as well as to individuals.

PRINCESS OF WANDS
(OR PAGE OF WANDS)

Traditional Interpretation

Personality. The Princess of Wands has a lively, energetic personality. She is sociable and friendly. She brings new life and vitality to the Querent's situation in her role as a supportive and faithful friend, or as a messenger who brings good news.

Situation. The card represents the Querent starting something new with enthusiasm and energy. It can mean

the arrival of good news, and new opportunities.

REVERSED
Personality. Here is a weak and shallow person who is full of a sense of her own importance; she is unreliable and inclined to break confidences and ignore privacy. She thinks she is very helpful and even popular, when she is really rather boring and iritating.

Situation. The Querent lacks energy and enthusiasm and is easily discouraged, either as a result of genuine obstacles, or through his own indecisiveness.

Interpretation for Relationships

Personality. If the card represents a person, she is probably an adolescent girl or a young woman exploring sexual relationships for the first time.

Situation. The start of a new relationship, or good news concerning a relationship, is indicated. Other possible interpretations are the arrival of love-letters or lively and innovative sexual activities.

REVERSED
Personality. She is an immature individual who brags about her sexual conquests but who has little real experience and is weak and unreliable.

Situation. Lethargy and timidity with regard to sex are indicated. Bad news concerning a relationship, or the arrival of an unhappy love-letter, may also be signified.

PRINCESS OF CUPS (OR PAGE OF CUPS)

Traditional Interpretation

Personality. Here is a quite and gentle person who is artistic and imaginative. Being introverted, she does not generally seek out company, but is always friendly and helpful if her advice is sought. Modest and sensitive, her talents, artistic skills, and possibly psychic abilities, may go unrecognized by others. She is a studious and thoughtful person who could be of great help to the Querent.

Situation. The Querent may find that this is a time for careful thought, reflection and quiet study. There may be an opportunity for him to develop artistic, creative or psychic skills, or to take up some new interest that involves reading or studying on his own. This card can indicate the awakening of latent talents.

REVERSED
Personality. This person has skills and artistic talents, but

lacks dedication. She tends to be lazy or frivolous, acting upon whims and failing to apply herself to worthwhile projects. She may have limited knowledge and skill in a number of areas, but her interests are too widespread for her to have acquired any great ability in one area. She needs to apply self-discipline in order to utilize her potential.

Situation. The Querent is missing some potentially helpful or positive aspect of his situation, possibly through a failure to recognize his own talents and to use them effectively.

Interpretation for Relationships

Personality. This card may represent a sensitive young lover who is very considerate towards her partner's feelings.

Situation. Gentle love and the expression of tender emotions are signified.

REVERSED
Personality. The card in its reverse aspect may represent a vain, flirtatious young woman who fancies herself as a lover.

Situation. Frivolous and flirtatious activity is indicated here. A love-affair looks promising but turns out to be shallow and unsatisfactory.

PRINCESS OF SWORDS (OR PAGE OF SWORDS)

Traditional Interpretation

Personality. She is an intelligent person, alert and far-sighted. She has a skill in seeing to the heart of any matter, and is decisive and resolute, especially when quick, responsible decisions are required. She is aware of many possibilities and alternatives and is always on the look-out for opportunity. There may, however, be an element of mistrust or suspicion here. Despite her sharp intelligence and ability to make rapid decisions, she is cautious and even furtive, wary of the possibility that others may intend her harm. She is helpful in resolving disputes where intelligence and cautious discretion are needed.

Situation. The Querent is in a situation which calls for level-headedness, quick thinking, and the need to make careful decisions. This card warns that it is important to be alert and cautious, but on the other hand, too much hesitation and lack of trust or faith could be a disadvantage. There is a need for balance and a proper sense of perspective in dealing with a delicate and unpredictable situation.

REVERSED

Personality. Here is a cunning and hypocritical person. Because of her own strong sense of insecurity and an awareness of her own weakness, she becomes scheming and devious in an attempt to build up a wall of defence around herself. She is good at seeking out weaknesses in others which she can exploit for self-gain, encouraging feelings of enmity between others which she can turn to her own advantage.

Situation. This is a difficult situation in which the Querent needs to be alert to possible dangers. Perhaps he has good reason to be cautious and suspicious; there may be unreliable, even malicious people around who will take advantage of him. On the other hand, this defensive approach could be inappropriate, especially if it continues for long. There may be a need to make important changes, either in the situation itself, or in one's own attitude, in order to relieve the tension here.

Interpretation for Relationships

Personality. An intelligent, cautious young lover may be represented by this card.

Situation. Discretion and delicacy with regard to a relationship or sexual matter is called for. The Querent must be cautious and use his tact and intelligence.

REVERSED
Personality. The reverse aspect of this card may represent a blackmailer or voyeur who will make trouble for the Querent.

Situation. The Querent should be wary of people prying into his relationships or sexual activities.

PRINCESS OF DISCS
(OR PAGE OF DISCS)

Traditional Interpretation

Personality. This is a sensible, reliable person who is hard-working and methodical. Though she has few ideas of her own, she is good at work of a routine nature where attention to detail is important. She may be a student or apprentice, or someone in a junior position in business. She makes a loyal friend or business acquaintance, practical, obliging, down-to-earth, and careful with money.

Situation. Small beginnings and firm foundations are the basis of future success. Hard work and study will bring results. It may be a time when, rather than bright ideas, dull, routine work is necessary. Employment prospects look good for someone who is willing to work hard and be conscientious and patient.

REVERSED
Personality. Here is a dull, rather pompous person, who is inclined to assert what little authority she has in petty and obstructive ways. She is slow, materialistic and basically lazy, tending to make heavy weather of any matter she undertakes. Lacking in any good ideas of her own, she resents other people more intelligent than herself, asserting herself wherever she can in a mean and tiresome fashion.

Situation. All the fun has gone out of the Querent's life. Bogged down by material worries or by a monotonous routine, he lacks the energy to make necessary changes for the better. A new outlook, a hard-earned holiday, a change of job or change of environment are needed here. A boring, frustrating situation may be bringing out all the worst, obstinate, selfish aspects of the Querent's own personality. Trouble with bureaucracy may be indicated.

Interpretation for Relationships

Personality. She is kind and friendly, slow to show her feelings, but capable of deep passion and very loyal to those she loves.

Situation. A good friendship could grow into a deeper relationship. Slow, steady progress in affairs of the heart will bring good results. The Querent should be wary of trying to hurry matters along too fast or of making sexual advances at too early a stage.

REVERSED
Personality. The card may represent a boring, pompous

lover inclined to narrow-mindedness and jealousy.

Situation. The Querent's sex life has ceased to be fun. Preoccupation with the mechanics of sex rather than concentration on developing a worthwhile relationship leads to selfishness and monotony which fails to provide satisfaction.

PRINCE OF WANDS (OR KNIGHT OF WANDS)

Traditional Interpretation

Personality. The person represented by this card uses his energy and enthusiasm for seeking new adventures and relationships. He is a charismatic, fun-loving person with a good sense of humour, but he is often unpredictable. People can be easily drawn into his company where they benefit from his warm and generous nature. If not the Querent himself, he will give the Querent new ideas and impetus for change.

Situation. The Querent is experiencing movement and change, and important goals can be reached. This card may indicate a change of environment in some sense, either moving home, changing job, travelling abroad or going on holiday.

REVERSED

Personality. He is unreliable and jumps to hasty judgements. He will start things he does not finish because his enthusiasm is too easily dissipated, and he has no staying power. His need for instant success makes him impatient and annoying to other people. Never around when he *is* needed, he interferes when he is not, causing confusion and chaos.

Situation. Here the Querent faces rapid change which is too fast to deal with — too many things are happening at once. He feels confused, and is possibly at odds with other people, experiencing stress and finding it hard to cope. He needs to slow down and deal with one thing at a time.

Interpretation for Relationships

Personality. This card may represent a very sexy, attractive and charming young man who would make a very exciting lover.

Situation. A lively sex life, new relationships, or the changing of sexual partners may be indicated.

REVERSED

Personality. He is someone who appears very charming but is unreliable and is inclined to be promiscuous.

Situation. Sexual energy and changeability tend towards reckless and promiscuous behaviour when this card is reversed. Fickle love, imprudent sexual experimentation and one-night stands are indicated.

PRINCE OF CUPS
(OR KNIGHT OF CUPS)

Traditional Interpretation

Personality. He is a calm and amiable person, sensitive, imaginative and artistic. He has an original and inventive mind, but may be easily bored and given to fantasizing. His arrival often heralds new ideas and opportunities. However,

because of his passive nature, he may have an unfortunate tendency to be influenced by others and be diverted from his own purpose.

Situation. New opportunities and ideas are available to the Querent at this time, particularly with regard to personal relationships, love and marriage.

REVERSED

Personality. He appears kind and pleasant on the surface, but is not to be trusted. His true motives remain hidden, while under the guise of friendship he may be using other people to further his personal schemes. Though he may not intend any real harm, he is prepared to resort to deception and trickery while pretending to co-operate with others, harbouring resentment and reluctantly agreeing to their demands, while secretly plotting retaliation. This could be the behaviour of a weak or timid person who is afraid to make his real feelings known.

Situation. Circumstances which appear positive may contain hidden pitfalls. There are dangers here which have not been recognized. Hopes may have been raised too high and difficulties ignored. The situation should be reviewed. A more realistic and cautious approach would be advisable.

Interpretation for Relationships

Personality. He is a very romantic young man with an idealistic view of love. He sees sex as a component of a loving relationship rather than a desirable end in itself.

Situation. This is an auspicious card for the Querent's love life, as already indicated.

REVERSED
Personality. The card may represent a deceitful lover whose intentions are other than they appear to be on the surface.

Situation. The Querent should be wary of being misled in matters of love. High expectations are likely to lead to disappointment.

PRINCE OF SWORDS (OR KNIGHT OF SWORDS)

Traditional Interpretation

Personality. This young man is capable of swift and forceful action. He is intelligent, resolute and practical in difficult situations. Where there is injustice, opposition, obstacles, or threats, he is good at finding quick and effective solutions. He may represent a strong friend or ally who will help the Querent in times of trouble. In situations where a more sensitive, emotional, or methodical approach is needed, however, the Prince of Swords may be more of a hindrance than a help, for he is lacking in patience and the ability to sustain effort for long periods of time.

Situation. Struggles and conflicts are imminent, but if the Querent has a direct, rational and decisive attitude here, he has a good chance of overcoming opposition.

REVERSED
Personality. Here is a strong, aggressive person whose impatient attitude makes him blundering and incompetent. He is full of show and bluster, but he achieves little result for all his effort, and his energy is often spent before anything is gained. He tends to start projects and leave them unfinished.

Situation. Patience and steady application are needed here. Hasty decisions, impulsive action, anger and confrontation will cause trouble and make unnecessary obstacles. The Querent should take a step back, review the situation, and plan carefully before he proceeds. It may be a situation where intuition, sympathy or tact is needed, rather than impulsive action.

Interpretation for Relationships

Personality. He may represent a young man who is forthright and virile but who lacks tenderness or subtlety. His intentions are honest and good, but he has difficulty in showing emotion.

Situation. The cards of the Swords suit in general are not very auspicious with regard to emotional matters. This card could signify a stormy relationship or conflicts with a partner.

REVERSED
Personality. The card in its reverse aspect may signify a selfish and bullying lover who even resorts to physical violence in extreme cases.

Situation. Arguments and conflict in a relationship are indicated. Further confrontation will be likely to aggravate problems.

PRINCE OF DISCS (OR KNIGHT OF DISCS)

Traditional Interpretation

Personality. He is a good-natured, reliable, gentle person who enjoys a quiet and simple life. He takes great pleasure in simple, quiet pursuits, his approach to life being rather plodding — slow but sure. Hard-working, generous, and always well-meaning, he has a calm, practical approach in everyday situations and generally achieves the straightforward and modest aims he sets himself. In times of stress and difficulty, however, his plodding, easygoing nature may find it difficult to cope when quick thinking or impulsive action is required.

Situation. This may indicate a time when very little is happening. There is no hurry; life's simple pleasures can be enjoyed at one's leisure. Slow but steady progress is indicated. Long-standing problems will be resolved, given time and patience.

REVERSED
Personality. This is an old-fashioned, conservative person, whose plodding approach is ineffectual and inappropriate to the circumstances in which he finds himself. He may appear weak, depressed and somewhat pathetic, but it is possible that these qualities have come about as a result of a reluctance or inability to adapt his outlook to changing circumstances. Someone who is clinging to the past, reluctant to give up old habits and an old way of life, may well display the characteristics of this card.

Situation. The situation calls for a different approach to the one the Querent is currently adopting. An easygoing, casual attitude is inappropriate here and methods which have worked in the past are no longer effective.

Interpretation for Relationships

Personality. He is a kind, warm-hearted, faithful lover who will provide security for the Querent.

Situation. A slowly developing relationship becomes deep and secure. Love and faithfulness are indicated.

REVERSED
Personality. If a person is represented, he is a very dull, uninspiring lover.

Situation. A relationship is making no progress and has become dull and stale. Obstacles to romance and marriage are indicated.

QUEEN OF WANDS

Traditional Interpretation

This woman is energetic, capable and sociable. She is quite able to run a home and pursue her own career, as well as engaging in hobbies and keeping a wide circle of friends. She is versatile, warm, sympathetic, helpful and generous. She is both independent and devoted to her family.

Queen of Wands

REVERSED
Well-meaning, but possibly selfish, she is inclined to interfere where she is not wanted. She tries to run things her way, is over-protective to her children, and believes that she is always right. She wants to feel appreciated and needed, when probably people would manage better without her interference.

Interpretation for Relationships

With her fiery Wands energy this woman is sexually active and passionate. She knows what she wants from a relationship and knows how to get it, but she is also a very dynamic and supportive partner. Despite her independence of mind, she makes a devoted wife and mother.

REVERSED
She is inclined to be prudish, disapproving of unconventional sexual behaviour. She may be inclined to interfere in other people's relationships and to adopt the attitude of a moral crusader against what she regards as sexual immorality. In her own private life she may be sexually inhibited or frustrated.

QUEEN OF CUPS

Traditional Interpretation

This woman is quiet and introverted, but her personality is very deep, and she has strengths which may not be immediately apparent. She has highly-developed artistic, intuitive, and possibly psychic skills. She may have an air of mystery and other worldliness about her which makes her appear at first sight to be dreamy and impractical. With regard to business and material matters she may not be very practical, for this is not an area where her talents lie; but she displays great strength of will and intelligence when her abilities are applied to artistic and creative pursuits, or to any emotional situation where her quiet sympathy and intuition are needed. She is a person who is very much in contact with her unconscious self and the inner needs of others, and she also knows how best to use this understanding for positive ends.

REVERSED

The reverse aspects suggest a frivolous, irresponsible personality. This woman will appear very charming and fun-loving and may have great physical beauty, but her charms are only superficial. She is vain and silly, and likely to be a fair-weather friend. In times of difficulty she is impractical and given to self-pity, too involved in her own interests and flights of fancy to be trusted to provide others with the support they need. Relying on her is likely to lead the Querent into trouble. This card can also indicate the negative or destructive effects of too much fantasizing — self-pity and idle day-dreaming can lead to disillusionment or lack of contact with reality.

Interpretation for Relationships

She is a romantic and sexually alluring woman whom men find extremely attractive. Because she is quiet and reserved she may appear aloof and unresponsive, but beneath her calm exterior she is capable of deep feeling. Sensitive and loving, she is very aware of the feelings and needs of her partner, and tries to satisfy these.

REVERSED
In her reverse aspect, the Queen of Cups is a fickle and flirtatious woman. She likes the attention of men because she is easily flattered, but she is unwilling to remain faithful to one partner. She is likely to lure a man into a relationship with her against his better judgement, only to desert him for a new lover.

QUEEN OF SWORDS

Traditional Interpretation

Traditionally this card represents a widow or lonely woman who has suffered pain and loss. She is intelligent and strong-willed, however, and her independent life-style may be of her own choosing. She is someone who has learned to be resilient and to cope well with problems and disappointments. She may be a brilliant and ambitious business woman or professional who has chosen a career rather than marriage and motherhood; or she may be a widow or divorcée who has learned from unhappiness and has become stronger as a result, living her new life with a greater sense of purpose.

REVERSED
This woman is ambitious and domineering. She is highly intelligent, but has little regard for the feelings and rights of others. She is stern, critical, impatient and selfish, demanding that everything be done in accordance with her own rigid requirements. She tends to be secretive and scheming, and is quite unscrupulous in the means she employs to further her own ends. The reverse aspect of this card can show someone whose experience of a life of hardship and suffering has made them cold, bitter and ruthless in an attempt to cope with personal unhappiness.

Interpretation for Relationships

Romance and sex feature very little in this woman's life, either through personal choice or as a result of bereavement. She may regard her career as far more important; possibly she has a dislike of sex or finds difficulty in showing love. On the other hand, she may be a lonely widow or divorcée who has been unwillingly deprived of sexual love.

REVERSED
In her reverse aspect she is a cold and embittered woman who is destructive in her relationships, unable to give or receive love, hostile to sex or to men in general.

QUEEN OF DISCS

Traditional Interpretation

She is a warm, sensuous woman who appreciates home comforts and likes an easy life. Affectionate and generous, she enjoys a good time and is always ready to share what she has with others. She is someone who lives very much in the world, who is closely in touch with nature and with the needs and feelings of those around her. She is associated with fertility, hospitality and an abundance of the good things in life. Her presence provides material and emotional security and a sense of well-being.

REVERSED

This woman is materialistic and unnecessarily concerned with outward appearances. Her suspicious, griping attitude and her airs and pretensions may well conceal a neurotic and insecure personality. Her apparent greed, displays of wealth, and personal aggrandizement may disguise a deep sense of inner worthlessness and dissatisfaction with herself, her relationships and her personal achievements. She generally represents a frustrated unhappy woman who is making trouble for the Querent in a bid to gain his attention, but her behaviour is likely to provoke annoyance rather than sympathy. Tact, firm kindness, and infinite patience are needed to deal with this woman whose own lack of confidence can make her very awkward and demanding.

Interpretation for Relationships

The Queen of Discs is a very sexy, voluptuous woman who is kind, warm, and generous, as well as enjoying all aspects of physical sex. She takes great pleasure in physical sensations and she also likes dressing up in sexy clothing and playing erotic games. Marriage and motherhood are very important to her, and having babies is intrinsic to her notion of sexuality and to her self-image as a woman.

REVERSED
In her reverse aspect she is unhappy in her relationship and sexually frustrated. She may feel that she is undesirable and unattractive, or feel that her partner is unable to satisfy her sexual needs. A strong desire for children she is perhaps unable to have may be an underlying cause of her frustration and low morale.

KING OF WANDS

Traditional Interpretation

This person is mature, responsible and accomplished. He enjoys being the witty and charming host. Strong-minded and strong-willed, he is also affectionate and generous to those in his circle. He makes a good father and husband. However, he may easily be irritated by the need to attend to details. He soon forgets failed ventures, quickly regaining his natural confidence and optimism. Where there are arguments and disputes he is good at giving advice without bias or favouritism.

REVERSED
Here is a man who has one rule for himself and another rule for everybody else. He is intolerant of other people's views and behaviour, believing that he always knows best. He is critical of the faults in others, but refuses to recognize his own faults. He prides himself on his own high standards, both practical and ethical, but because of his inflexible and unsympathetic attitude, he often causes more harm than good. Although he may be well-intentioned, his narrow outlook and unyielding response to the needs and feelings of those around him create many difficulties in his relationships with them.

Interpretation for Relationships

Sexually he is extremely virile and masculine. He makes a passionate and witty lover and a devoted husband and father. In a relationship he always tries hard to see his partner's point of view, and is fair and loyal. He is receptive to the needs of his partner, but is also sexually adventurous and likes to try out new sexual activities and techniques.

REVERSED
In his reverse aspect the King of Wands is a man who tends to impose a patriarchal authority in his relationships. He sees himself as head of the household, regards himself as superior to women, and is insensitive to the needs of others. He is very proud of his own masculinity, but his attitude towards sex is likely to be puritanical and conservative. He may be afraid of his own sexuality, guiltily concealing sexual perversions and visiting prostitutes while giving the

outward appearance of being a respectable family man.

KING OF CUPS

Traditional Interpretation

Here is an intelligent man who has wide knowledge and experience, particularly of an academic, intellectual or artistic nature. He is likely to be cultured, highly educated and professional. Because of his sophistication, however, he could appear cold and unapproachable. He may represent some professional person, such as a lawyer, doctor or business man, whose advice will be of importance to the Querent. When involved in close personal relationships, on the other hand, this is a man who will feel ill at ease. Although he cares about others and likes to be supportive, he finds difficulty in expressing his own feelings, which he often experiences as embarrassing complications. Dignified and reserved, his real strengths lie in his great wealth of knowledge, refined sense of taste and a thoroughly professional outlook.

REVERSED
He is a cool, elegant man, ambitious and scheming, who involves others in projects which further his own interests

but are often detrimental to the interests of others. He may represent an untrustworthy business partner or professional person whose advice will lead the Querent into difficulties. In personal relationships he is selfish and unfeeling and has no scruples about the distress he causes others while furthering private schemes. He uses his intelligence, education and social standing for purely selfish ends.

Interpretation for Relationships

As already indicated, the King of Cups is uneasy in his close personal relationships. He is very difficult to live with, appearing cool and aloof, and he conceals his real feelings which he may not even understand himself. He is embarrassed by what he sees as sentimentality, and is unlikely to show affection openly. He probably has a low sex-drive and prefers intellectual activities to sex and emotional involvement. He certainly does not mean to be unkind, but his cool behaviour is part of his nature and he is unlikely to change. He may enjoy the company of women, but as intellectual companions rather than lovers.

REVERSED
He is a dishonest man who uses love and sex simply as a means of furthering personal schemes and to bring him personal wealth and power. As a lover he is cold and domineering. He is inclined to see sex as a commodity which can be used to promote status and business success. He may involve other people in vice and sexual scandal while his own reputation remains unsoiled.

KING OF SWORDS

Traditional Interpretation

This is a strong, intelligent powerful man. He may represent someone whose professional advice is sought by the Querent, especially someone who will give advice in legal or business matters. He is sharp-witted, ambitious and ready to assert himself when necessary. He is someone who likes to be in a position of authority or to be working for himself. He resents being restricted by tradition, close

personal ties or the requirements of other people. He prefers to start new projects and go his own way. He has innovatory ideas and a strong drive which usually bring him success in life; but as he is inclined to be cold and authoritative, he may be less successful in personal relationships than he is in business or work.

REVERSED
When this card appears reversed in a spread, the Querent should beware; there is almost certainly some unpleasant domineering person in their life, be it a selfish father, husband or lover, an exploitative employer, devious business man or professional person with whom the Querent has contact. Whoever he is, this man is out for all he can get, and timid, good-natured people are an easy target for him. He is intelligent and aggressive and can turn very nasty on occasion. The best way to deal with him is to stand up to his bullying; to attempt to compromise or appease him is likely to be playing into his hands. A calm, firm and decisive approach is best here.

Interpretation for Relationships

In personal relationships the King of Swords is likely to be cold and unemotional. He may be attractive to women because of his undoubted masculinity and his air of cool authority, but he can make a harsh and unloving husband and father. Unlike the King of Cups, there is no softness under this man's hard outward appearance; he always responds on an intellectual level and is lacking in spontaneity. He is fundamentally a man's man and may hold women in low esteem.

REVERSED
The reverse aspect of this card is particularly unpleasant in regard to personal relationships, since this man can be a tyrant around the home. He intimidates those around him and can resort to violence and sadism in order to assert his authority. He is ruthless and scheming and may use sex to exploit people for his own ends.

KING OF DISCS

Traditional Interpretation

Here is a practical man who has achieved success and stability in his life. He is secure and contented, able to enjoy what he has built up for himself and willing to share what he has with others. Like all the characters of the Court cards in the suit of Discs, he is someone who enjoys the good things in life, who is satisfied with what he has, and is generous towards others. He is not especially intelligent, but his achievements have come about through hard work and steady progress which has brought him material success as well as emotional satisfaction. Possibly he is someone who is good at making things with his hands; certainly his skills are of a practical nature and he has a plain, common-sense attitude, as opposed to any striking intellectual ability. He is a gentle, kindly man with a calm, generous outlook.

REVERSED

Here is a man who judges success only in material terms. He will take any opportunity to make money and may resort to dishonesty and fraud at times. Even when he has the material success he craves, he is still likely to be dissatisfied because he is unable to enjoy the finer things. His grasping, miserly attitude and his materialistic outlook have cut him off from other people, from nature and from life's simple pleasures, so he has become insensitive, distrustful, greedy and dull. Again, as with other reversed Court cards, the person we see here may not be morally bad so much as deeply unhappy. The good qualities of the King of Discs have become blocked, so that in seeking success and security he has attained only material wealth and none of the satisfaction and joy that ought to go with success. He is like King Midas whose golden touch only caused him pain and loneliness.

Interpretation for Relationships

He is a gentle, kind man who will be a good husband and lover. He has a sensuous, affectionate nature, and though he may not be especially virile he enjoys all sensual pleasures. He probably likes and admires women and is able to sympathize with their point of view. He also understands children very well, is patient and gentle with them, and makes a good father. Domestic life and security are very valuable to him, and he is likely to have a conventional view of love, sex and marriage. He may be lacking in all the obvious charms that women find attractive, but he is a good, honest, loyal man who will be successful and contented in a long-term relationship where other more glamorous and attractive men may sadly fail.

REVERSED

In his reverse aspect he is a dull, unpleasant person with vulgar or even gross sexual tastes. In relationships he is clumsy and crude. He sees sex as an end in itself and is likely to pursue sexual gratification with little regard for morality or the feelings of others. He is likely to enjoy pornography and rude jokes because he is unable to rise above this level of sexual appreciation. Despite his undiscriminating sexual indulgence, he remains unfulfilled and unhappy because he does not realize that sex cannot be a substitute for real love.

CHAPTER SIX
THE PIP CARDS

THE ACES

The Aces (representing a singularity or unity) embody the full force and character of the suits to which they belong; each Ace, then, has the pure, undivided qualities of the element of the relevant suit. The Ace of Wands represents the element of Fire and signifies in a completely unadulterated form the qualities associated with this element; likewise, the Ace of Cups stands for Water, the Ace of Swords for Air, and the Ace of Discs for Earth. Also, as the leading card in each suit, the Aces are associated with beginnings, births, new projects and inspiration at the start of anything.

ACE OF WANDS

Traditional Interpretation

Wands represent the element of Fire, which is associated with intuition, creativity, enthusiasm, activity, ambition, impulsive action, excitement, new ideas and masculine virility. The Wand is an obvious phallic symbol and embodies certain aspects of the masculine principle. The suit of Wands is often associated with career, business projects and new ventures; but when a card of this suit appears in a spread, it can represent any plans, ideas or activities in the Querent's life to which the fiery quality of the Wands is applicable. The Ace, as the leading card, represents the full power, enthusiasm, creative energy, ambition and driving force of the suit.

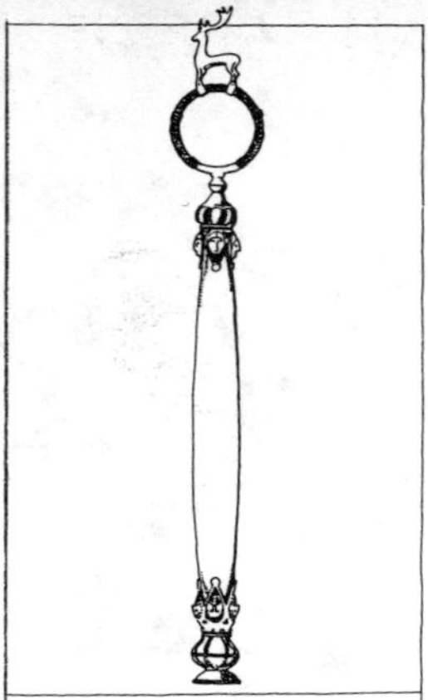

ace of wands

REVERSED
When this card is reversed, some of the drive and energy of the upright meaning is still present, but because this power is now misdirected it is likely to be wasted and spent too soon. Weakness, lack of energy, lack of ideas, and ineffectual action is likely to be the result. The Querent may feel tired, drained, unenthusiastic, frustrated and powerless, because he is wasting his effort in futile schemes which have led him to adopt a negative or even destructive outlook.

Interpretation for Relationships

This card represents male virility. New relationships and an energetic sex life may be indicated. It may also signify that the Querent is taking the initiative in a sexual relationship.

REVERSED
Impotence or lack of sexual energy may be indicated. Alternatively, the Querent may be putting his energy into activities or relationships which are unsatisfying. Frustration and an inability to attain sexual satisfaction are signified.

ACE OF CUPS

Traditional Interpretation

Cups are associated with Water — a passive, feminine, nurturing element. The suit of Cups, therefore, represents emotion, sensitivity, close personal relationships, quiet, contemplative experiences and artistic, poetic or psychic ability. The Cup may also be seen as a symbol of the womb or vagina; it represents the feminine principle. The Ace of Cups signifies love, peace and contentment, emotional security, happiness, fulfilment and inspiration. In some cases it can specifically represent a birth or a marriage. It can also signify artistic talent, or a spiritual experience. More usually it represents warm feelings of love and caring, and the joy and sense of security that comes from a fulfilling deep relationship or a close friendship.

REVERSED

When the Ace of Cups is reversed in a spread, it represents sorrow, pain, loss, and an unhappy relationship. Problems and disappointments regarding marriage and relationships may be indicated. Melancholy emotions, tears and sorrow, despondency, depression and a sense of loss or loneliness are the reverse aspects of this card.

Interpretation for Relationships

Love and sexual satisfaction are provided by a warm, secure relationship. This is a very favourable card with regard to all aspects of the Querent's love life. Engagement, marriage or pregnancy may be indicated.

REVERSED
A disturbed relationship, lack of love, sexual deprivation and depression are signified when this card is reversed. Because of a lack of emotional fulfilment, sexual enjoyment is not possible either, so that even if sexual opportunities are available they are likely to be unhappy experiences.

ACE OF SWORDS

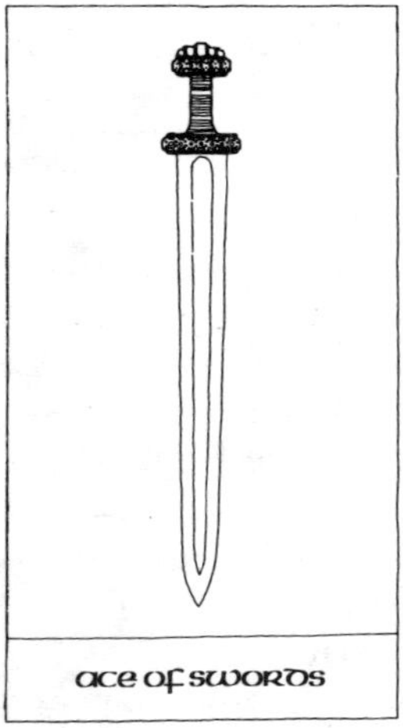

Traditional Interpretation

The suit of Swords is associated with the element of Air and the faculty of intellect. This suit is also associated with pain and conflict, and with the masculine qualities of power, law and order. The Sword is a phallic symbol representing aspects of the masculine principle. The Ace of Swords embodies the strong, forceful qualities of this suit. It stands for intelligence, authority, logical thinking, strength of will, justice and organization. It can indicate either a clear-headed, rational attitude in the Querent, or a situation in which order, organization, justice and integrity are paramount. In some cases it can signify legal matters. When the card is upright, this is a sign that justice and reason will prevail.

REVERSED
When the Ace of Swords is reversed, it represents the negative, destructive aspects of power. If it denotes the Querent's own attitude, this is a warning that he is misdirecting and misusing his intelligence, skill and authority, disregarding the feelings of others and perhaps his own emotional needs. If the card represents a situation in which the Querent is involved, it stands for injustice, cruelty, unfair dealings and problems with the law or any other system of authority.

Interpretation for Relationships

This card can represent a voracious sexual appetite, sex without love, or recourse to the law to resolve problems issuing from a broken relationship. It is not, therefore, a good card regarding relationships. It may indicate male domination and control in a relationship.

REVERSED
Male domination, violence, exploitation of women or children, rape or sexual injustice may be signified. In its reverse aspect, this is a card of sexual crime and the worst manifestations of male sexual power.

ACE OF DISCS

Traditional Interpretation

The suit of Discs represents the element of Earth, which is associated with security, fertility, work and money. Along with the Cups, it is regarded as a feminine suit, and is associated with traditionally feminine aspects of life — the home, family, and practical everyday matters. The Ace of Discs stands for emotional and material security, enjoyment of the good things in life, and sensual pleasure. It

can represent the acquisition of material wealth, but more generally it stands for comfort and satisfaction, which may result more from a secure family life and sense of one's own inner worth than from material prosperity. It can also indicate that the Querent has a warm, generous nature, or that he has a deep appreciation of beauty or a love of plants and animals.

REVERSED
The reverse aspects of the Ace of Discs are insecurity, discontent, and a preoccupation with material things. Problems with money, emotional insecurity, or a materialistic oulook, can all be represented by this card. It can also indicate that the Querent is unable to enjoy life or to appreciate what he has. Someone who is unusually anxious, self-conscious, puritanical or cynical, or possibly physically ill, may have this card appear reversed in a spread.

Interpretation for Relationships

Voluptuous sensual pleasure and the enjoyment of physical sex are indicated. Security within a relationship and love expressed through sex are also signified by this card. Complete sexual fulfilment, appreciation of the beauty of the human body, and acceptance of one's physical nature and needs may all be indicated.

REVERSED
Failure to find love and security in a relationship, sexual guilt, shame and disgust, an inability to gain sexual satisfaction, sterility, a puritanical attitude to sex, or physical illness that disrupts one's sexual activity may all be signified by the reverse aspect of this card. Alternatively, it can indicate concentration on the physical side of sex and sexual technique to the exclusion of love and emotional needs, or an over-indulgence in sex, leading to boredom and physical debility.

THE TWOS

The number Two signifies duality and the relationship between one thing or person and another. Ideas of the combination of two compatible, or conflicting, personalities, energies or principles, and the balance of two equal forces, are signified by the number Two cards in the Minor Arcana. These are modified by the elemental qualities corresponding to each suit.

TWO OF WANDS

Traditional Interpretation

As Wands are associated with energy, ambition and career, this card is one of achievement and ambition. This signifies the successful completion of the first stage of some project and the opportunity for further progress. Initial problems may have been overcome, and there is reason for optimism, but the duality of the Two suggests that there is also some element of unease or conflict present. The Querent may be weighing up decisions, planning what to do next and contemplating obstacles ahead. This card can indicate promotion, or the fulfilment of an ambition, but this success may also be tinged with regret, self-doubt and a questioning of one's aims and ideals. In some cases a business partnership may be indicated.

REVERSED
When the card is reversed, the negative aspects are inclined to outweigh the positive, so that achievements are accompanied by feelings of doubt, discontent, lack of enthusiasm, and a sense of futility. It can indicate a sensation of anti-climax when a long-awaited goal has finally been reached, or recognition that one's past aims were futile or that one's values were misplaced. In business arrangements it can indicate disagreement with colleagues or the ending of a partnership.

Interpretation for Relationships

The early stages of a personal relationship have been successful, but the Querent is wondering how to go on from here. He may already have attained all he desired at first and is now wondering whether deeper involvement is possible or even desirable with this particular partner. This card may represent the kind of feelings some people experience after the first few months of marriage when the romantic atmosphere of early love has passed and a different kind of love has begun to replace it. It may also represent the feelings some people have after many years of marriage, when the relationship needs to take a new direction if it is to continue to be meaningful to the parties involved.

REVERSED

The Querent experiences a feeling of futility about his relationship. Anticipated love and security have not materialized, or his sex life has become dull and meaningless. The card suggests that he has serious misgivings about a personal relationship and wonders if it can possibly continue.

TWO OF CUPS

Traditional Interpretation

This is the suit of the emotions, so the Two of Cups represents a close personal relationship between two people. A love affair or a friendship is usually indicated, but the card can also represent the ending of a conflict or rivalry. The qualities signified by this card are love, friendship, sympathy, mutual understanding, tolerance, forgiveness and co-operation. An engagement or marriage may be indicated, or perhaps the making of a new friendship, or the start of a new relationship.

REVERSED

Quarrels, conflict and the clash of personalities are indicated when this card is reversed. It can signify the end of a relationship, the breaking of an engagement, or a divorce. It can also represent arguments and misunderstandings within a long-standing relationship. Lack of consideration, the breaking of trust or an agreement, and hasty destructive actions and impulses which cause distress and are later regretted, can all be represented by the reverse of this card.

Interpretation for Relationships

The coming together of two people in love is represented by this card. Engagement or marriage may be indicated. The starting of a new romance or the deepening and continuation of an existing relationship can be signified.

REVERSED
As already indicated, the reverse aspect of this card does not bode well for a relationship. Sexual incompatibility may be signified, along with difficulty in understanding and fulfilling a partner's sexual needs and desires.

TWO OF SWORDS

Traditional Interpretation

In the suit of Swords, associated with power, intellect, and aggression, the number Two card signifies an uneasy balance between opposing forces and ideas. It usually represents a tense situation in which conflict is likely to arise and in which peace is maintained only by the exercise of discretion and self-restraint. Arguments and trouble may seem imminent, though at present the situation has been stabilized. The opposition and threat to the status quo probably comes from outside in the form of another person who is in an antagonistic relationship to the Querent; but the conflict in some cases may come from within, when the Querent has desires and commitments which sway him in opposite directions.

REVERSED
When this card is reversed, it indicates that the unsteady balance has been tipped and conflict has arisen. The attempt to be calm, rational and impartial has failed and now there will be strong expressions of anger and resentment on either side. In extreme cases there may be violence or cruelty, but the distress is more likely to be caused by strong words, obstinacy and injustice. The reverse aspect of the Two of Swords, therefore, shows two irreconcilable viewpoints and the conflict that arises at the point of contact when reason and restraint have broken down.

Interpretation for Relationships

The Querent's close personal relationship is unstable and volatile, and is likely to deteriorate into arguments and conflict at any time. The sexual side of the partnership may be strained and lacking in spontaneity. Alternatively, this card may represent a conflict in the Querent's own feelings towards sex and relationships.

REVERSED
Severe conflict in a relationship is highlighted. An inability to see the other's viewpoint, irreconcilable differences, marital disputes, a broken engagement, separation or divorce may be indicated.

TWO OF DISCS

Traditional Interpretation

The concept of balance and equilibrium applies also to the Two of this suit, and, as the Discs are concerned with material and emotional security, and practical affairs, this card represents a sensible approach to life. When it appears in a spread, it indicates that the Querent is a capable person with an optimistic outlook, who is able to enjoy life at present and who is coping well, even in the face of difficulties. This card represents enjoyment of the present moment, an easygoing, accommodating attitude, and the ability to cope with problems if they arise.

REVERSED

The reverse aspect of this card indicates fluctuation of attitude and purpose. The Querent is likely to be moody and restless, happy one day and miserable the next; he may find it hard to maintain an interest in anything over periods of time long enough to achieve what he wants. Indecision, silly, impulsive and immature behaviour may be represented by this card; on the other hand, the Querent may simply feel confused and incompetent to deal with current problems.

Interpretation for Relationships

A casual, happy-go-lucky attitude to love and sex is indicated. The Querent enjoys the pleasures of the moment without making firm commitments for the future. At present he is contented and sexually satisfied. His approach is practical and he has no romantic delusions.

REVERSED
The Querent's love life is turbulent and unpredictable. He feels his relationships do not last long enough for them to develop in the way he would like. His attitude to sex may be immature or irresponsible. Sexual frustration leads him to do silly and impulsive things which worsen his existing problems.

THE THREES

The number Three represents the idea of creation. A third entity reconciles the opposition of the Two and the bridge between irreconcilable opposites, but it can also be seen as the result of the union of opposites, as a child is produced from the sexual union of a man and a woman. Thus the number Three signifies the completion of the first stage, and the creative energy from which progress, new direction and growth can take place. The number Three is also, importantly, associated with divine power and spiritual creative energy; the Deity has often been thought of as having a threefold nature, not only in Christianity, but also in Eastern religions and Goddess-based religions. Three, therefore, is the number of divine creation and spirituality, as well as of regeneration and creativity in the mundane sense.

THREE OF WANDS

Traditional Interpretation

As the suit of Wands usually relates to business and enterprise, this card represents the successful beginning of a project and the laying of plans for the future. It indicates

that schemes regarding career and life-style will be successful. There is an abundance of ideas, energy and opportunities, and prospects for the near future look optimistic.

REVERSED
There is some difficulty in putting plans into practice. The Querent may find that good ideas tend to remain only as dreams and the opportunity to make them a reality either fails to arrive, or he is too slow or timid to avail himself of it. Possibly there is a gulf between his hopes and ambitions and what is actually practicable at this time.

Interpretation for Relationships

Opportunities to develop a relationship are open to the Querent, but it is not clear how the situation will progress. The Querent has hopes and plans with regard to love and a prospective sexual partnership, which appear to depend to some extent upon good fortune for their fulfilment. Only time will tell how this will turn out, but the signs look very favourable.

REVERSED
Sexual fantasies and delusions of romance are indicated. The Querent sees the object of his desire but has no realistic

idea of how to attain his goal. Timidity may be holding him back; on the other hand, he may be in love with someone who is not free to reciprocate.

THREE OF CUPS

Traditional Interpretation

This card typically signifes the growth of a relationship, a secure home and the starting of a family. More generally, it can apply to any satisfying relationship and to the birth in a metaphorical sense of spiritual understanding, or the emergence of some creative work which is of great value to the Querent's emotional life. The card indicates a time of happiness, inspiration and good fortune.

REVERSED

What could be a happy situation or a rewarding relationship is being spoilt by selfishness or inhibition. There is a lack of generosity and tolerance, and a reluctance to discuss or share problems. This card typically represents relationships in which people are using one another and are reluctant to express love or affection. It can indicate marital problems, troubled family life, and, occasionally, problems relating to pregnancy.

Interpretation for Relationships

As already indicated, this card represents the flourishing of a relationship founded in love. Marriage and pregnancy are indicated, as are celebrations concerning these important events. Wedding festivities or great joy at the birth of a child may be signified.

REVERSED
Sex without love, or an unloving or exploitative relationship may be indicated. The physical inability to have children, or social obstacles to starting a family are other possible interpretations.

THREE OF SWORDS

Traditional Interpretation

As we have seen, the suit of Swords is associated with power, ambition and intellect, and for this reason the cards in this suit have, on the whole, unfavourable meanings. The cold ruthless energy of the Swords, though needed on some occasions, can often have unfortunate and destructive implications. In the Three of Swords, therefore, the combination of the two Sword entities to produce a third, has violent and disturbing consequences.

This card represents pain, sorrow, and destruction. Very occasionally it may even indicate death when it occurs together in the same spread with other cards of misfortune (e.g. Death, The Tower, or other Sword cards). The Tarot reader should be careful, though, never to predict death for, however skilled the reader, there is always a chance of being mistaken, and in any case the Querent will be caused alarm and distress, which must be avoided.

On the positive side, the violent or disturbing changes signified by this card may be necessary in clearing the ground for new and better developments in the future.

REVERSED
When reversed, this unpleasant card represents pointless destruction, or a miserable situation which has continued for a long time. Feelings of hostility, continual arguments and the wilful adoption of an obstructive or negative attitude may be indicated here. There is not much hope for improvement, especially if this situation is a long-standing one, unless someone makes determined steps towards changing it.

Interpretation for Relationships

The destructive ending of a relationship, causing pain and turmoil, is indicated. A relationship has irretrievably broken down and can now only be a source of pain and sorrow. Separation or divorce are signified. In the circumstances, this may be the best possible outcome, though the Querent probably does not appreciate this at the time.

REVERSED
The Querent continues to struggle on with a destructive relationship. There is little hope here for improvement and he may have to recognize that the relationship must end. Alternatively, the reverse aspect of this card may show that the Querent is still suffering from the aftermath of a painful relationship break-up.

THREE OF DISCS

Traditional Interpretation

As the suit of Discs is associated with money and practical matters, the product represented by the number Three in this suit is the product of labour. This is the card of employment and hard work. The work here is usually work that is done for someone else — an employer or client — rather than work towards a personal project. When this card is upright, it indicates that the work is done well and meets with approval from others concerned.

REVERSED
This card still signifies hard work when it appears reversed, but now it seems likely to be a thankless labour. The Querent may meet with disapproval or criticism which he resents, and there is a general atmosphere of dissatisfaction attached to the working situation. Possibly the Querent dislikes his job or has awkward relationships with people at work. He may feel at present that his contributions are not appreciated and that he is not valued or respected as he should be.

Interpretation for Relationships

Working hard at a relationship will bring the desired

rewards. This card indicates that practical considerations must be taken into account too; love is not always enough. The practical work of setting up a home and planning carefully for the needs of one's partner and family are vitally important. Care and diligence in establishing a good home and setting firm foundations to one's relationship will ensure happiness in the future.

REVERSED
The Querent feels that he ought to model his private life in accordance with other people's requirements. Pressures of work, family or material worries disrupt his love life and sexual activities. If this situation is temporary and unavoidable, it will have to be tolerated, but if there is no sign of improvement the Querent should make changes. Love and personal relationships should be a priority and not made subject to outside requirements. Alternatively, the reverse aspect of this card may indicate that the Querent feels he has put a lot of effort into a relationship and that his partner does not properly appreciate him. A more open discussion of feelings and clear expressions of love may be required.

THE FOURS

Four is the number of stability, order, and firm foundations. It suggests a square, the four cardinal points, the four seasons, the four elements, and is the number associated with matter and the material world. It therefore has a calming, pacifying effect upon the force and energy of the masculine suits of Wands and Swords, whereas its effect upon the quieter feminine suits of Cups and Discs is more likely to produce stagnation and rigidity.

FOUR OF WANDS

Traditional Interpretation

The fiery energy of the Wands, in combination with the number Four, produces a calm, stable atmosphere in which

there is nevertheless scope for creativity and free expression. This card represents a pleasant, orderly environment together with an enthusiastic, optimistic outlook. It may indicate celebrations or a holiday, but it can also appear in a spread when the Querent is engaged in some creative or artistic pursuit, or possibly even in painting and decorating his home.

REVERSED
The restrictive nature of the Four tends to outweigh the Wands' energy when the card is reversed. This can indicate personal inhibitions or a fear of expressing oneself because of criticism or intolerance from others. There is tension here between bright, enthusiastic ideas and a narrow, conservative outlook. The conflict could be within the Querent himself; alternatively it may be the case that his own attitude is at odds with the view of conservative and narrow-minded people around him.

Interpretation for Relationships

Spontaneous expressions of love, and freedom from sexual inhibitions are indicated. The card represents a pleasant, secluded environment which is favourable for the development of romantic and sexual relationships — perhaps a romantic holiday, a honeymoon or second honeymoon.

REVERSED
Restraints are put upon the Querent's sexual freedom, and his love life is inhibited. Circumstances are unfavourable for love-making, possibly because of lack of privacy or because the Querent has a narrow, conservative attitude towards sex. Disapproval from other people, and restrictive social mores, may be making it hard for him to engage in the kind of relationship he desires.

FOUR OF CUPS

Traditional Interpretation

The passivity of the Cups, combined with the stability of the Four, produces dullness and apathy. This card, therefore, signifies boredom and dissatisfaction. There is a sense of being stuck in a rut or of feeling fed up with an existing situation, even if that situation has certain advantages. The Querent needs to make some changes, and perhaps engage in new activities, in order to bring variety and interest back into his life.

REVERSED
The boredom and apathy described above can be a major problem when the card is reversed. Self-indulgence, self-pity

or depression may be indicated, and the Querent may feel lethargic or have a fatalistic attitude to his predicament. Causes and possible solutions to the problem may be suggested elsewhere in the spread.

Interpretation for Relationships

The Querent's love life has become extremely boring. Lethargy or exhaustion inhibits enjoyment in sexual activities and there may be a failure to attain orgasm. The Querent may have a pessimistic view of his relationship or of personal relationships in general, feeling that no improvement is possible and that the situation will continue indefinitely, but this need not be the case if he makes an effort to bring about positive changes.

REVERSED
Extreme lethargy and boredom are indicated. The Querent either despairs of his relationship or has ceased trying to find pleasure in sexual activity. General depression may have contributed to sexual problems, or possibly sexual excesses have led to satiety and exhaustion.

FOUR OF SWORDS

Traditional Interpretation

The calming influence of the number Four has the effect of blunting the unpleasant, sometimes destructive qualities associated with the Swords. This card signifies an opportunity for rest and recuperation following a time of pain and struggle. It can represent, specifically, recovery from an illness, a stay in hospital, or a much-needed holiday. More generally it indicates that recent problems or worries have been, or will shortly be, alleviated.

REVERSED
Unpleasant experiences, conflict or illness, have had a deeper, longer-lasting effect than described above. Reversed, this card represents withdrawal or isolation as a result of, or solution to, an earlier problem. The Querent may feel unhappy or resentful about this, even though the withdrawal or isolation could have been of his own choosing; he may have a feeling of being banished, cut off from others or rejected.

Interpretation for Relationships

The Querent has removed himself from the pressures of a relationship or from sexual activity in order to recover from a distressing experience. This card may indicate that the Querent is recovering from a broken relationship or has had to refrain from sexual activity temporarily for medical reasons. Chastity, celibacy or the conserving of sexual energies may be signified.

REVERSED
The Querent feels rejected or banished, or has had to withdraw from involvement in a difficult relationship. The cessation of sexual activity or the necessity for restraint of one's sexual appetite may be indicated. This is possibly connected to a medical problem.

FOUR OF DISCS

Traditional Interpretation

The stabilizing effect of the Four upon the earthy, material

character of the Discs, produces a security so complete that it is in danger of becoming an obstacle to any further growth or change. Both material and emotional security are indicated here, but it is likely to be accompanied by an over-cautious, unimaginative outlook. This sort of stability and security could come as a welcome relief after a time of stress or upheaval, but as a permanent way of life it could become stifling.

REVERSED

When reversed, this card suggests someone who is so concerned with holding on to what he has that he is afraid of any change or innovation. Fear of failure or loss has led the Querent to adopt a timid, defensive, suspicious stance, unwilling to take any risks or to make any changes. He may even be prepared to maintain a bad or miserable situation, so fearful is he of inadvertently making it worse by trying to improve it. In fact, he may have little to lose and much to gain by simply taking a chance once in a while.

This card can also signify an emotionally cold or miserly attitude; an unwillingness to show affection or to share with others.

Interpretation for Relationships

The Querent's relationship is very secure and stable, but

this may be restricting or lead to dullness at times. He may be over-cautious and unimaginative in his love life, and fearful of change in his partner. This card may signify a clinging or over-protective relationship.

REVERSED

The Querent is fearful of taking risks and this inhibits him in developing relationships. He may try too hard to cling on to a partner, ironically causing the breakdown of the relationship in so doing. Afraid of rejection, he is reluctant to show love or to participate in the sharing which is necessary for a good relationship. He unwittingly shuts himself off from love and affection and is fearful of allowing himself sexual release.

THE FIVES

Five is the number of struggle and uncertainty. The stability of the Four is upset by adding the number One to it. The Fives, therefore, represent the arrival of problems, conflicts and disappointments which upset a potentially favourable situation.

FIVE OF WANDS

Traditional Interpretation

The optimism and energy of the Wands is sufficiently powerful to compensate for the unpleasant features of the number Five. The card indicates that there may be problems, arguments and obstacles to be overcome, but they are likely to be part of one's normal routine; annoying, rather tiresome incidents which interfere with the smooth running of things, but which the Querent is quite capable of dealing with. Such problems may be time-consuming and a nuisance, but they are generally nothing serious, and one may even experience a sense of exhilaration in overcoming them.

REVERSED
Set-backs, obstacles and disagreements of the kind described above are more troublesome when the card is reversed. The Querent may even have an unpleasant encounter with someone who actually intends to mess up his plans. Although nothing especially disastrous is signified, there could be some nasty moments and petty squabbling here, which the Querent would do best to try and avoid. Nothing is to be gained by getting caught up in such matters or in pandering to the whims of such trouble-makers.

Interpretation for Relationships

Quarrels and squabbles between lovers are indicated. Competition for love and sexual favours, and obstacles to love may be signified. Sexual bragging among boys or young men is another possible interpretation. The problems here are unlikely to be serious, however, and may be more in the nature of teasing or game-playing than causing any major disruption of a relationship.

REVERSED
The quarrels or obstacles are more problematic when the card is reversed. Competition for sexual partners, jealousy and trouble-making may be signified. The Querent should

ignore the activities of anyone who is trying to meddle in his relationship or to break up his engagement or marriage.

FIVE OF CUPS

Traditional Interpretation

The emotionality of the Cups suit combined with the idea of upsetting a secure situation, which is associated with the number Five, makes this a card of disappointment and loss. As with all the Fives, however, no major problem is indicated here, although the loss or disappointment may be experienced as worse than it actually is because the Querent is taking an unnecessarily pessimistic view, brooding on his misfortune and ignoring the good things that he still has. Not all is lost; there is some reason to be optimistic, even though matters have not turned out as well as one might have hoped.

REVERSED

A real and inevitable loss is indicated here, which causes the Querent sadness and regret. There may be a painful disappointment, the end of a relationship, a bereavement in some sense, or the ending of something which has played an important part in the Querent's life. Only the passage of time will alleviate the distress naturally felt in such circumstances.

Interpretation for Relationships

The fading of love and the decline of a relationship may be indicated. The Querent is dwelling on the love that he has lost and the missed opportunities for romance; his unsatisfactory love life and lack of sexual fulfilment preoccupy him so that he fails to see positive aspects of his situation or ways in which it might improve. Troubles in marriage, the end of a love-affair or the frustration of hopes in love may also be indicated.

REVERSED
The failure of love, the end of a relationship or the loss of a sexual partner may be signalled. The Querent feels sad, lonely and bereaved, and it will take considerable time to recover from this loss.

FIVE OF SWORDS

Traditional Interpretation

The instability of the Five, in combination with the aggressive power of the Swords, makes this a card of humiliation and defeat. The Querent has lost face or has in some way been shown up as weak and silly. Possibly he has been overpowered by a strong, domineering or superior person who has made him feel small and inferior. There is unlikely to be anything that can be done to rectify this situation; the Querent must come to accept the fact that someone has got the better of him. It is fundamentally pride that is at stake here, however, rather than any substantial or physical danger to the Querent's self or well-being.

REVERSED
The Querent experiences a painful and humiliating defeat. As with the other Fives, the unpleasant and disappointing aspects of the upright meaning are more marked when the card is reversed, while the positive features are unlikely to be present. The Querent may well have encountered a bully or someone who deliberately meant him harm, or he may have become the victim of someone acting in a spiteful or dishonest way.

Interpretation for Relationships

The Querent feels humiliated and defeated in a matter of love. This may be the result of a partner's domineering attitude or unfaithfulness. Social embarrassment may be involved, as when someone is ashamed to acknowledge the fact that their relationship has broken down. Within a relationship, ridicule and intimidation may be indicated.

REVERSED
The Querent has been painfully put down, degraded, rejected or treated sexually in a humiliating way. His partner may have left him for another lover and he feels he has been made to look foolish and weak. The reverse aspect of this card signifies a more painful and damaging defeat than when the card is upright, possibly leading to loss of self-esteem, persistent feelings of degradation, and sexual insecurity.

FIVE OF DISCS

Traditional Interpretation

The struggle, uncertainty and disappointment of the number Five manifests itself in the suit of Discs as material and emotional insecurity. This is a card of poverty and adverse material circumstances. It indicates problems with money and sometimes unemployment. More generally it represents the lack of something for which the Querent feels a strong need. The poverty here can be understood in an emotional or spiritual sense, as well as a material one. However, help may be closer at hand than the Querent imagines. Sharing his problems with a sympathetic person who can give moral support may provide the comfort and security he is in need of at this time.

REVERSED

The adverse circumstances, sense of insecurity, financial problems or unemployment may continue for longer when the card is reversed, sapping the Querent's energy and making him passive and fatalistic about his situation. This attitude must be combatted if any improvement is to be made, and a change of tactics or a shift of priorities may be in order if a deterioration into a vicious circle of frustration and despair is to be avoided.

Interpretation for Relationships

The Querent feels an acute lack of love and sexual fulfilment. Present relationships fail to provide emotional security, and the Querent may be lacking in any close personal relationship at all. As a result he feels deprived of love and sex. This situation is likely to be temporary, however, and new opportunities for romance may already be at hand.

REVERSED
Deprivation of love and sex has persisted for longer when the card is reversed, leaving the Querent feeling hopeless, unlovable and unattractive. This tendency to despair may actually be exacerbating the problem, and positive steps towards forming the relationship he desires are called for if the situation is to improve.

THE SIXES

The number Six stands for balance and equilibrium; the concepts of fairness, rewards, and the consequences of past actions and events which bring benefits in the present are associated with these cards.

SIX OF WANDS

Traditional Interpretation

Success, triumph and achievement which are the results of past efforts can now be enjoyed. Care and patience will be rewarded. If the Querent has been waiting for news of the outcome of any matter, good news is to be expected when this card appears in a spread.

REVERSED
Success is delayed and problems continue. There may be lack of communication and misunderstandings involving other people. The Querent may be anxiously waiting for news which has been delayed, and expected or hoped for success has not arrived.

Interpretation for Relationships

The Querent's hopes of developing a good relationship are fulfilled. A patient, tactful approach to forming a friendship or initiating sexual relations brings the desired result. Engagement or marriage after a long period of waiting is now possible. Good news in a letter from a loved one may also be indicated.

REVERSED

Lack of communication or misunderstandings in a relationship are represented. There are delays to romantic and sexual fulfilment. Engagement or marriage is postponed. A long-awaited love-letter or news of a loved one fails to arrive.

SIX OF CUPS

Traditional Interpretation

A past relationship is renewed or in some way brings pleasant consequences in the present. An old friend or lover may have reappeared unexpectedly in the Querent's life; past experiences, especially those which are happy and which are fondly remembered, have some bearing upon present circumstances and may be a help or comfort to the

Querent at this time. A past act of kindness to a friend may be returned in gratitude.

REVERSED
Unpleasant events in the past may still be having a lingering effect. The Querent is in some sense living in the past, regretting that the good times have gone or that a relationship has ended; childhood memories and sentimental feelings may be affecting his behaviour now in an adverse way. A morbid dwelling on the past could result from fear of the future or could indicate dissatisfaction with one's present way of life, while at the same time being a means of evading a course of action which needs to be taken now.

Interpretation for Relationships

A past lover returns unexpectedly and the relationship is renewed. This could possibly represent reconciliation in a marriage after a period of separation. Alternatively the Querent may be simply remembering past love-affairs and finding pleasure in happy memories.

REVERSED
A past lover returns and makes trouble for the Querent. Alternatively the Querent is thinking of past love-affairs or

broken relationships, regretting past actions or wishing that he could return to the times of love and sexual fulfilment he once knew. A sentimental longing for lost romance is indicated.

SIX OF SWORDS

Traditional Interpretation

Many of the Sword cards have unfortunate or sad meanings, so despite the generally good meaning associated with the number Six, the Six of Swords has a slightly melancholy atmosphere about it. The suggestion here is that the Querent has suffered and may suffer again, but there is nevertheless a sign of an improvement in circumstances. Past problems and unhappiness are receding, and though there may still be difficult times ahead, the outlook is more optimistic than it may have been for a long time. The worst at least is certainly over. Occasionally this card indicates a physical move into more congenial surroundings and may suggest travel abroad.

REVERSED
Immediate problems have been resolved, but unsatisfactorily. An attempt at an easy solution is only postponing

trouble. The Querent may be refusing to confront his problems in the hope of avoiding further pain, but this will only lead to recurring difficulties. A permanent solution should be sought.

Interpretation for Relationships

Distressing and bad experiences of love or sex are now receding into the past and the Querent is able to recover from a period of suffering. Possibly the Querent is rebuilding his life after a broken relationship and is now able to look ahead to a brighter future. Alternatively the card may show the Querent overcoming problems in a relationship which will improve from now on, and moving to a better environment may be connected to this.

REVERSED
The Querent is postponing dealing with problems in his relationship in the hope that they will go away, but this is unlikely. A frank, open approach and honest discussion with a partner may be painful or embarrassing, but this is the only real way to deal with recurring difficulties of an emotional or sexual nature.

SIX OF DISCS

Traditional Interpretation

This card represents balance and fairness with regard to money and security. The giving or receiving of gifts may be involved here. The Querent may receive money or help from a kind and generous person, but could equally be feeling generous himself. This card can also represent the paying of a karmic debt, the expression of gratitude, or a fair and just action resulting from pleasure in one's own good fortune and a desire to share what one has with others.

REVERSED
The Querent has suffered some loss or theft, which may be a loss of money or material possessions, but can also be the loss of personal security, love or friendship. The loss may have been due to his own carelessness or lack of foresight, but is more likely to be an injustice resulting from the selfish action of another person.

Interpretation for Relationships

The giving and receiving of love and sexual pleasure is indicated. Here is a loving, supportive relationship between equals which endows the Querent with a secure and generous outlook. There is much caring and sharing. The giving of romantic gifts may be shown.

REVERSED
The loss of love or the loss of a sexual partner, possibly through unfaithfulness, is indicated. The Querent feels he has been treated unjustly and that love has been dishonestly stolen from him.

THE SEVENS

The number Seven is associated with wisdom, morality, supernatural powers, divine justice, and fate. For instance, there are Seven Virtues and Seven Deadly Sins; the Seven Sisters, Seven Pillars of Wisdom, or Pleiades in ancient mythology, were the divine judges of men. Seven is a number therefore that is thought to have great mystical and magical significance.

SEVEN OF WANDS

Traditional Interpretation

The combination of the special powers and wisdom of the Seven, together with the energy of the Wands, represents the ability to overcome opposition and obstacles and to face a challenge with courage and enthusiasm. This card indicates that the Querent's abilities may be put to the test now or in the near future, but he is perfectly capable of coping, and may even derive some sense of pleasure and satisfaction in doing so. If the Querent is going to be participating in any sort of competition, test or examination, this is an auspicious card that indicates success.

REVERSED

The Querent feels daunted in the face of problems, or backs down from a challenge. He may actually possess the ability to cope quite well, but lacks confidence in himself and so has missed a good opportunity. He probably feels embarrassed or ashamed at his own failure and recognizes that he is letting himself down. Having greater faith in his own ability could be an important factor in ensuring success.

Interpretation for Relationships

The Querent is faced with a challenge in his love life. Obstacles must be overcome or rivals defeated before he can attain the love he desires. The Querent has a positive attitude, however, and is confident in his ability to succeed. Love that is hard-won appears all the more desirable to him.

REVERSED
The Querent is timid in the face of obstacles and feels defeated when his amorous advances are rejected. Possibly fear of rejection prevents him from trying to form relationships at all. He may lack confidence in his sexual performance, aggravating sexual problems because of his fear of failure.

SEVEN OF CUPS

Traditional Interpretation

The Querent is confronted with several different choices or courses of action and finds difficulty in deciding which one to take. The emotional and psychic qualities associated with the Cups, in combination with the magical quality of the Seven, create a potentially hazardous influence in this card which, without the more sobering effect of reason and practical knowledge, can evoke confusion and pointless day-dreaming or fantasizing. When this card appears in a spread, therefore, it may suggest that the Querent has many ideas, impressions and unconscious desires but lacks the organizational ability to make practical plans or to come to a decision on a particular matter. It is necessary to consider goals and possible courses of action very carefully to avoid making unfortunate mistakes here.

REVERSED
The sense of bewilderment and the tendency to fantasize rather than take action is stronger when the card is reversed. There is a danger that the Querent may continue to dream about what he might do if circumstances were different, instead of taking more notice of how matters really stand and planning more carefully ahead. There is a strong suggestion here of a serious gulf between the Querent's aspirations and his actual present circumstances.

Interpretation for Relationships

The Querent has romantic dreams and desires but is unsure of how to fulfil them. Many possibilities seem open to him, but at present he cannot decide how to act. Possibly he would like to act out some of his sexual fantasies, but is unsure how to go about this, or is doubtful of the reaction of his partner.

REVERSED
Wild sexual fantasies and romantic delusions have taken the place of real relationships and an active sex life. The Querent feels safer day-dreaming or looking at erotic pictures or literature than taking steps to develop a real-life relationship. This may be because he is despondent and has given up hope of ever finding real satisfaction.

SEVEN OF SWORDS

Traditional Interpretation

The intelligence and foresight often associated with Swords, together with the mysterious qualities of the number Seven, make this a very interesting card. It

indicates that the Querent is able to take a clever, possibly unconventional, course of action to deal with an existing problem or in order to secure certain future advantages for himself. Emphasis here is on doing the unexpected and forestalling trouble by planning ahead. Intelligent, decisive, unorthodox action is likely to bring worthwhile rewards at this time. Circumspection and timely precautions will yield more fruitful results than outright confrontation with people and forces stronger than oneself.

REVERSED
The Querent is likely to lose a good advantage through timidity and lack of foresight. He may encounter problems as a result of taking too conservative and cautious an approach.

Interpretation for Relationships

Furtive and stealthy sexual activity is indicated, or the use of skill and cunning in engineering an amorous encounter. Things and people that obstruct the development of a relationship are cleverly evaded rather than confronted directly. An unconventional attitude to love and sex may be indicated and the Querent has the determination to behave according to his personal values regardless of possible disapproval from others. An elopement may also be signified.

REVERSED
The Querent is unwilling to take a risk or to behave unconventionally in a matter concerning love or sex, and so misses a valuable opportunity. A desire to behave in an open and honest manner brings him up against people who want to frustrate his romantic intentions, and he feels too timid to defend himself against them.

SEVEN OF DISCS

Traditional Interpretation

Continued effort and the exercise of practical skills will bring good results at this time. The Querent should not despair or give up too soon if there are delays or if the situation looks unfavourable. Past work has not been in vain, and perseverance now is well worthwhile. There may be an unexpected stroke of good luck in the near future.

REVERSED
The Querent has allowed depression and despondency to prevail over good sense and the will to succeed. A bad

situation has been allowed to grow worse and it may be impossible now to reverse the process. Opportunities have been lost and possible success abandoned, and now the Querent may be suffering problems that were largely self-induced. It may be too late to salvage anything from this situation, and the Querent would probably do best to learn from this experience and to move on to new projects.

Interpretation for Relationships

Perseverance with a relationship that looks unpromising will bring favourable results. The Querent should not be discouraged by apparent failure in his love life as a new sexual partner or changes within an existing relationship are soon likely to provide him with what he desires. An existing friendship may unexpectedly develop into a sexual relationship.

REVERSED
A deterioration in the Querent's relationship or lack of success in finding a suitable sexual partner has led him to despair and to wonder whether it is worth persisting. He may be depressed and indulging in self-pity, no longer trying to improve the situation. Persistent sexual dysfunction that has led to a feeling of hopelessness and a lack of self-confidence may be indicated.

THE EIGHTS

Eight is the number of completion of one stage and progression on to the next. As the number Four multiplied by Two, it carries the stability and wholeness of the Four, together with the notion of using this stability as a basis for future development.

EIGHT OF WANDS

Traditional Interpretation

The notion of completion together with the energy of the Wands signifies a swift and satisfactory conclusion to any

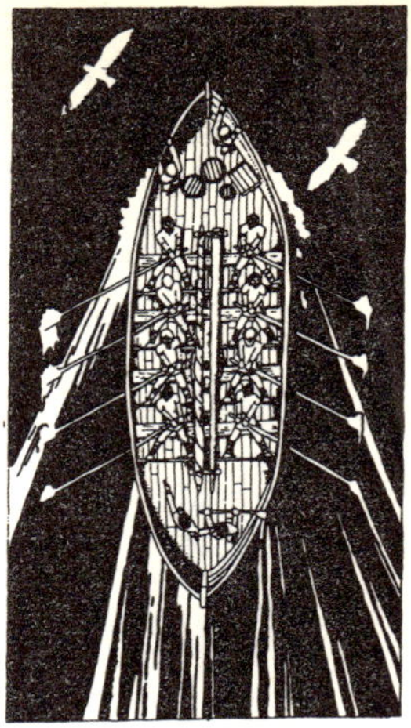

matter in hand. Delays will come to an end and there will be much excitement and activity. Events, once set in motion, will run their course with little further intervention or effort on the Querent's part.

REVERSED
Energy is wasted by acting in the wrong way at the wrong time. A swift succession of events occurs which causes difficulty for the Querent and which is outside his control. Problems arise as a result of hasty actions and sudden developments which happen too quickly for the Querent to cope with them.

Interpretation for Relationships

Swift developments in matters of love and sex are indicated. Suddenly falling in love, being swept off one's feet by love or passion, quick seduction or hasty sexual encounters may be indicated. The implication is that the Querent will probably have little time for consideration — passions and sudden impulses will provoke him to take unexpected courses of action.

REVERSED
The Querent makes ill-considered and hasty decisions with regard to his love life. Much energy may be wasted in

pursuing relationships that lead nowhere. Sexual problems related to haste and speed such as hurried love-making that is unsatisfactory, or premature ejaculation may also be indicated.

EIGHT OF CUPS

Traditional Interpretation

The ideas of completion and progression to a new stage, together with the emotion of the Cups suit, suggest the end of old relationships and the beginning of new, perhaps deeper relationships. The Querent may be feeling dissatisfied with an existing relationship or way of life and is thinking of making changes. The making of new friends, the widening of social horizons, a change of job or a move to a new home may be indicated. Whatever change or development is represented here, however, it will be something instigated by the Querent and wanted by him as part of a need for personal growth and progress. He may feel some doubt or uncertainty about his decision, but overall he is likely to feel that this is the right thing to do.

REVERSED

The end of relationships and changes in one's way of life are still indicated when the card is reversed, but there is a it also represents completion, the result, or the final stage. This final stage of development may bring certain problems with it, but past experience and methods of coping become important here and are an intrinsic part of the meaning attached to the Nines.

NINE OF WANDS

Traditional Interpretation

A strong position and a determination to succeed in spite of obstacles and past difficulties is represented by this card. The Querent may have had many set-backs and may have suffered, but he is able to use the foundation which he has managed to build up through past experiences to face the future with optimism and strength. In many respects his present attitude is defensive and wary, and he is probably well aware of the difficulties that may be in store, but there is also much positive energy here, and what has already been achieved places the Querent in a fairly strong position from which to advance.

REVERSED
Past difficulties have made the Querent suspicious and over-defensive. Consequently he may have a tendency to be

obstinate, reluctant to make any compromise or to change his attitude or behaviour, even when he is shown to be in the wrong, as he is afraid of appearing weak or of being manipulated by others against his own interest. This inflexible attitude is likely to become a handicap as the Querent is unable to adapt to new situations where a novel approach is required, and it will also alienate him from others who are as likely to be potential allies as the enemies he fears they may be.

Interpretation for Relationships

After heart-break and disappointment in love, the Querent tries to remain optimistic and looks forward to better relationships in the future. The Querent learns from a bad relationship in the past and has a more positive approach to making a future relationship successful.

REVERSED
The Querent's attempts at being positive and practical with regard to some emotional or sexual matter have failed and his attitude now appears obstinate and selfish. Obstinate persistence in a relationship or in one's sexual approach in order to prove a point is unlikely to bring the desired results.

NINE OF CUPS

Traditional Interpretation

Stability and advancement in the emotional realm of the Cups makes this a card of comfort, contentment and well-being. A warm, generous and hospitable outlook is also suggested here, the enjoyment of good personal relationships, love and friendship, as well as comfortable material circumstances being indicated. This card may also show that the Querent has a generally optimistic, kindly nature, caring much more about having a pleasant time, helping others and enjoying the good things in life, than brooding over worries and difficulties which may impinge and cause trouble from time to time.

REVERSED
The contentment of the upright meaning becomes smugness and self-satisfaction when this card is reversed. The Querent may be complacent about a matter which is not as secure as he imagines, overlooking some important details when work still needs to be done. Vanity, self-congratulation and the according of too much importance to superficial appearances could be laying up trouble for the future. All may not be as well as it seems, and possibly the Querent is not as popular with others as he believes.

Interpretation for Relationships

Contentment and satisfaction with one's love life and sexual relationship is indicated. The Querent is kind, caring and affectionate towards his partner, and much love and generosity is shown between them. In their sex life the Querent is concerned to give physical pleasure to his partner and is gentle and considerate.

REVERSED
The Querent may be smug and complacent about his relationship, failing to perceive his partner's real feelings. Vanity about one's sexual prowess or personal attractiveness may be indicated, or perhaps the unwise choice of a partner on the basis of outward appearance or sexual attraction alone.

NINE OF SWORDS

Traditional Interpretation

The aggression and intellect of the Swords gives the Nine of this suit an almost diametrically opposite meaning to that of the Nine of the gentle and emotional Cups suit. The Nine of Swords indicates that the Querent is still suffering from the aftermath of past adverse experiences and has acquired a morbid and pessimistic outlook, brooding on worries and imagining the worst. It should be emphasized that the pain and anxiety in this card, though it originates from very real difficulties and unpleasant experiences, is greatly aggravated by the Querent's own thoughts and fantasies. This is very much a card of mental anguish and depression, and shows a mood or outlook that the Querent has grown into, probably as a result of past hardship. Comfort lies in the fact that, although circumstances may still not be particularly good, they are actually better than they may seem at present, and what the Querent might fear is in fact unlikely to come about.

REVERSED

When this card is reversed, the depression and anxiety have probably persisted for a long time, and the danger here is that the Querent may have got into a vicious circle in which fears are feeding on themselves. The real problem is not so much the unfortunate circumstances in which the Querent may find himself, but his own state of mind, which makes any subsequent problem he may face many times worse than it need be. Severe despondency, morbid fantasies, and possibly clinical depression could be indicated, and the Querent certainly needs help and support from others in order to cope with these feelings.

Interpretation for Relationships

Demoralization and a lack of confidence in one's attractiveness or sexual desirability is indicated. The Querent may be suffering after the break-up of a relationship and feels that he will never love or be loved again. Brooding thoughts and fantasies about sex and relationships plague the Querent. He may also be troubled by worries about what other people may be thinking about him; he is afraid of scandal and gossip about his love life.

REVERSED
Deep sorrow and depression after a broken relationship or a bereavement are indicated. The Querent feels completely isolated from love and affection. Alternatively, severe anxiety about sex, sexually transmitted diseases or sexual scandal may be signified.

NINE OF DISCS

Traditional Interpretation

The Nine, in connection with material and practical concerns associated with the Discs, signifies security and success resulting from past effort. Now is the time to enjoy the fruits of one's labours. Peace, comfort, relaxation and material well-being are indicated, but as with the other Nines there are also some negative undertones here. The suggestion is that the Querent may have had to struggle to get to this point, may have had to make some sacrifices along the way, and perhaps still feels that present good fortune is only temporary. The overall impression, however, is of success, pleasure, and rest that is well-deserved, and

past difficulties may simply make the Querent more appreciative of all that he has now.

REVERSED
The Querent's present fortunate circumstances, achievements and well-being are ill-founded. Past mistakes and misdeeds are likely to bring unfortunate repercussions. The Querent may have a guilty conscience about some matter which disturbs his peace of mind and threatens his present security. This card may be taken as a warning that he should try to rectify his errors before it is too late. It may be a time for re-evaluation of one's priorities and to recognize that compromising one's own integrity is too high a price to pay for gaining certain advantages which in reality may not bring the lasting security that they seem to offer at first sight.

Interpretation for Relationships

The Querent has had to struggle and work hard to attain the love and security of the relationship he now has. A wealth of sensual pleasure and emotional fulfilment is indicated, and also the time and leisure to enjoy sexual experiences.

REVERSED
The Querent's relationship is not as secure as it seems. He should be wary of temptations to behave dishonestly;

unfaithfulness, or deception in matters of love may be indicated.

THE TENS

As the final pip card in the suit, the Ten signifies a conclusion or summing up of what has gone before; but the number Ten can also represent a group or community of people, especially family or close friends. It should also be recognized that our system of numerals has Ten as the base — that is, we number from one to nine, and then start the whole sequence again, in numbers of two digits each. Ten, therefore, is the first number in the second sequence, and so can be seen as a beginning as well as an ending. Also, being one more than Nine — which can be seen as a final or completing number — it carries the negative connotation of being one too many, which is a meaning particularly evident in the Wands and Swords suits.

TEN OF WANDS

Traditional Interpretation

As Wands is the suit of ambition, ideas and struggle, the meaning of the number Ten is to be interpreted in connection with one's projects, interests, ideas, ambitions and business activities. There is therefore the indication that the Querent is engaged in the completion of some projects and the beginning of others; but the concept of 'one too many', associated with the Ten, is the overriding impression here. The Querent is attempting to do too much at once, taking on new work and responsibilities while still very much engaged in bringing other matters to a successful conclusion. The advice must obviously be to do one thing at a time, finishing what needs to be finished before starting anything new. With matters as they stand at present, all the Querent's projects and concerns will suffer if he is overworked and burdened with worries. It may be time for other people to take over some of the responsibility, and the Querent should be happy to entrust others with a few of the many jobs he is trying to do all by himself at the moment.

REVERSED

Again, the Querent is engaged in too many activities at once, but the reversed position of the card suggests that the problem is one that has been endured for a long time or that he has brought upon himself unnecessarily. Interference in the affairs of others, lack of trust in other people's abilities, or a determination to assert control over others or to manipulate matters to one's own advantage are possible interpretations. The Querent may have difficulty in working with others, in delegating authority or in making compromises to accord with other people's wishes. A more tolerant, relaxed and trusting approach is needed.

Interpretation for Relationships

The Querent feels burdened by the responsibilities of his relationship and is troubled by an excess of emotional or sexual demands made upon him. He may be trying to satisfy the emotional or sexual needs of more than one person and is experiencing stress as a result of this. An excess of sexual activity in trying to meet the needs of one particularly demanding partner may also be signified.

REVERSED
The Querent finds his responsibilities oppressive. His sense of duty, and possibly an element of mistrust towards his partner, makes him assert personal control in the relationship, but this has now become tiresome and exhausting. An unjustified sense of responsibility for his partner's total well-being or a desire to assert authority or to organize other people's private lives, are alternative interpretations.

TEN OF CUPS

Traditional Interpretation

In the emotional sphere represented by Cups, the Ten signifies happiness, contentment and the fulfilment of one's deepest hopes and wishes. As with other Tens, the family or a group of people may be represented by this number, which suggests that the Querent's happiness is to be found in his relationship with this group of people. As already mentioned, however, the Tens can also bear some negative connotations, even when the overall meaning is good, and it is possibly the case that the joy and fulfilment shown here is marred in some way. One member of the group, perhaps the Querent himself, may not be entirely satisfied with the situation, in spite of the almost idyllic perfection which is at first sight apparent in this card.

REVERSED
A potentially happy situation is disrupted by some annoying or unforeseen happening, or by the attitude of one member of a social group. Either the Querent, or a close friend or relative, is seen as a trouble-maker, or maybe the problems of this individual have destructive repercussions in the lives of other people with whom they interact. Alternatively, this one person may appear to be the cause of the problem, when really he has become the scapegoat for the troubles and frustrations of the rest of the group. This card reversed generally shows clashes of interests and personalities, especially within a family.

Interpretation for Relationships

The perfection of a relationship, a blissful married life and the establishment of a family are indicated. All aspects of the Querent's emotional and sexual needs are provided for, but to some extent this may appear too good to be true. As already mentioned, this card may signify some slight or concealed dissatisfaction in a situation that to all outward appearances completely satisfies the Querent's desires.

REVERSED
The potential for a contented family life and satisfying relationships is undermined by the discontent of one family member. Arguments with adolescent offspring about their relationships and sexual conduct may be indicated. Adolescent sexuality disrupts family life.

TEN OF SWORDS

Traditional Interpretation

The ending or completion, with a certain negative association as already described, which applies to the Ten, has even more unpleasant overtones when it is combined with the destructive power of the Swords. This is sometimes seen as a card of dire warning, portending

disaster and ruin. Again, the number Ten suggests that people other than the Querent are closely involved in this situation. The Ten of Swords can be seen as representing the worst, most painful point of a crisis, but it also indicates that problems are coming to an end; matters can get no worse than this, and an improvement must follow. Despite its ominous appearance, therefore, this card offers hope of an end to struggles and suffering, and the chance of a brighter future.

REVERSED

When the card is reversed, this indicates that, though circumstances are bad, worse is yet to come. An ending may seem imminent, but this is illusory. There may be a resurgence of past problems, and a troubling matter is likely to be prolonged. The Querent should be prepared for this, and not rely on false hopes which will make the situation seem even more frustrating and depressing than it already is.

Interpretation for Relationships

Destructive emotions or the breakdown of a relationship have unpleasant repercussions for other people indirectly involved. This card could indicate, for instance, that the Querent's extra-marital affair destroys his marriage or that children or other family members are very upset by his divorce. Alternatively the Querent may be one of the people whose lives are disrupted by the relationships and sexual conduct of someone else.

REVERSED

The kind of problem associated with the meaning of this card when upright is recurrent or persistent when the card is reversed. The destructive effects of a bad relationship have repercussions in the lives of others for a long time. Alternatively, problems which seem to have been resolved arise again. For example, unfaithfulness persists, promises are broken, or a relationship which was difficult in the past breaks down again after a period of apparent improvement. Whatever the problem, the unpleasant effects are felt by a group of people, such as a family.

TEN OF DISCS

Traditional Interpretation

The practical, material and emotional themes of the Discs make the Ten of this suit a card of security, family support, and the emotional fulfilment of family life. The influence of one's family and upbringing upon one's values, life-style, and both material and emotional security, are represented here. When the card is upright, the influence is usually a good one, although it may be recognized that some price has to be paid in terms of autonomy and personal power in order to enjoy this support and security. More specifically, the card may appear in a spread when the Querent has received, or is about to receive advice, help or financial assistance from relatives and close friends. A legacy, in either a literal or metaphorical sense, may be signified.

REVERSED
When this card is reversed, the family influence, whether it is understood to be in terms of attitudes, values, upbringing, material support or the behaviour of certain family members, is overall a negative one. The Querent may be burdened by commitments to others, by aspects of his upbringing, or by family problems which concern him at present. Occasionally, problems arising from a death, or quarrels over a will are indicated. Close friends may be represented too, rather than blood relatives.

Interpretation for Relationships

Love, security and sexual fulfilment within traditional family life are indicated. A social occasion involving the family, such as a wedding or christening, is a possible interpretation. Strong family ties and a commitment to a traditional way of life are signified; an arranged marriage or a partnership that involves strong family support may also be represented by this card. As with the other Tens of the Minor Arcana, however, the Querent may have mixed feelings about this support from his family, sometimes regretting the lack of freedom and independence.

REVERSED
The negative influence of a family background interferes with the Querent's love life or his attitude towards sex. Possibly his family disapproves of his relationship, or he has sexual problems or inhibitions as a result of his upbringing. The Querent has difficulty in resisting these unpleasant influences, but he must try to do so if he is to have a private life of his own.

BIBLIOGRAPHY

Barrett, Clive, *The Norse Tarot*, Aquarian Press, 1989.

Cavendish, Richard, *The Tarot*, Michael Joseph, 1975.

Crowley, Aleister, *The Book of Thoth*, Samuel Weiser, 1969.

Douglas, Alfred, *The Tarot*, Penguin, 1973.

Huson, Paul, *The Devil's Picturebook*, Abacus, 1972.

Lawrence, Theodor, *The Sexual Key to the Tarot*, Citadel Press, 1971.

Pollack, Rachel, *Seventy-Eight Degrees of Wisdom* (2 vols), Aquarian Press, 1980.

Sharman-Burke, Juliet, *The Complete Book of Tarot*, Pan, 1985.

Waite, A.E., *The Pictorial Key to the Tarot*, Rider, 1971.

Walker, Barbara G., *The Secrets of the Tarot*, Harper & Row, 1985.

INDEX